CURMUDGEONISM
A Surly Man's Guide to Midlife

KELLY CRIGGER

GRAYBEARD PUBLISHING

First Published in 2014 by Graybeard Publishing LLC

ISBN: 978-0-9912382-3-1

Printed in the United States

Cover Design and illustrations by Thomas Hunt

Edited by Jennifer Mench

ACKNOWLEDGMENTS

No one reads acknowledgments except the people being acknowledged, so you should probably move on to the good stuff if I don't know you. There's nothing to see here except an old man getting misty about his man friends. Still here? Good on ya. This book is dedicated to all the wonderful friends, compatriots, and manly men I've known over the years or at least the magnificent, weird bastards who helped forge this blob of shit into a true curmudgeon. It's a long list and they may not all be surly, but they all taught me something at some point. There are no women in this dedication not because I don't respect my wife, my mom, my sisters, or my aunts, but because this book is all about being a surly middle-aged man and dedicating it to women would be like dedicating the USS Arizona to Japan. It's just not right. I will probably never live that down, but that's part of being a curmudgeon. Therefore this is dedicated to:

My step-father Gary Colonna; the black belt curmudgeon of the highest order. He can verbally lash you to the mast and whip your spirit with guilt until you beg for mercy but also has the professionalism to stop when he sees your soul is defeated and weeping. As a kid I could never find a flank on his defenses but now that I've grown up I'm glad he held me to such high standards. It took me a lifetime to appreciate how his grumpy outlook on life was actually a crystal clear filter on the way people behave and how in the end they'll just disappoint you. Thanks Pop. This book is truly written in your honor.

My family Don Crigger, John and Stephen Colonna, Gary and Delk Oden, Alec Hereford, Sam Crichton, Tommy Waterworth, John McGriff, Scott Delmain, Bill Sinnett, Bob and Jason Heffelfinger, Mark DeHarde, and my wild and wonderful West Virginia cousins John, Eric, and Danny Cady.

The high school buddies who shaped my formative years-Dave Sandefur, Tim Lee, Chris Chiles, Rob Beck, "The best man in a pinch" Mike Mielke, Dave Mielke, Mitch Young, and Randy Harrington.

The Jayhawk homies who taught me what the word "priorities" really means-Tim "BFFs before it was cool" Rodgers, Frankie Laster, Mike Beatty, and Chad Hinrichs.

The incredible Army mentors who taught me wrong from right and this from that-General JD Thurman, MG Ed Reeder, MG Robert Williams, MG Jeff Buchanan, BG William E. King IV, Colonel Stan Clemens, Colonel Kevin Higgins, Dr. (LTC Retired) Chuck Bass, and First Sergeant Terry Brown.

The guys who truly shaped me by proving time and again what brotherhood means, my Army buddies- Sean Kirschner, Shawn Perry, Tim LeDonne, Mike and Robbie Ladd, Daryl Collins, Al Roach, Blaine Hedges, Thamar Main, Tony Demarco, Pat O'Brien, Dean Klopotoski, Eric Berdy, Dave Dunphy, Matt Mock, Steve Smith, John Cushing, John Hermeling, Rob Horne, Matt Redmond, Todd Nethery, Jamie Dyke, Mike Marti, Conor Cusick, Scott Mitchell, Todd Walsh, Tom Duncan, Brent Parker, Brett Reister, Sergio Dickerson, Bill Barnett, Dallas Dunn, Alex Lovasz, Jefferson Varner, Karl Cockrum, Matt Barnes, Carlos Vega, Mike Bolluyt, Otto Liller, Haydn Hungerford, Todd Emoto, Dennis Heaney, Jamie Burns, Guy Lemire, Sean Hoyt, Bryon Galbraith, Tom Disy, Al Moore, Tim Mertsock, and CGSC Class of 2003 Seminar 11C.

The incredibly talented and unapologetically American Ranger Up crew and friends who continually find creative ways to tell life it hits like a bitch: Nick Palmisciano, Tom Amenta, Tim Kennedy, John Tackett, Garrett Schemmell, Rob Ulrey, Greg Drobny, Toby Nunn, Doc Bailey, Brett Kreiss, Jack Mandaville, Rob Halford, Tim O'Donnell, Mike Schlitz, Elias Donker, Keith Toy, Brad Elllingson, Matt Burden, Mark Seavey, Todd Vance, and a slew of other veterans/writers I'm probably forgetting but I shouldn't because they are intimately familiar with live ammo.

The rapscallions of MMA-Greg Jackson, Ricardo Liborio, Reed "The Fight Scientist" Kuhn, Eric "More Intensity" Talent, Mike "The greatest editor ever" Carlson, Jorge "El Conquistador" Rivera, Brian Stann, Donald "Cowboy" Cerrone, Aaron Riley, Kenny Florian, Matt Phinney, Tim Burrill, Scott Rehm, Mark DellaGrotte, Ben (not Knowles) Fowlkes, Dann "Fuck KU" Stupp, Chuck "Flat Cap" Mindenhall, Donovan Craig, Bear "Boy Band" Frazer, Chad Robichaux, Todd Vance, Tom Gerbasi, Ben Goldstein, Kris Perkins, Matt Larsen, Jeremy Botter, Mike Straka, Luke Thomas, John Morgan, Ariel Helwani, Jason Moles, Matt Roth, Josh Carey, Danny Acosta, and Mike Dolce.

The guys who let the old man play, the Washington Irish Rugby Football Club-Steve "Duma" Johnson, Whitney Stowell, James Thompson, Ian Pope, Joe Edwards, Chuckie Goldston, Luke Hammock, Mark Opdyke, Brendan Worley, and Derek Keane.

The California Crew who let me marry their little sister-Jamie Melton, Brian Sharp, Jay Hall, Jeb Burns, Noah Logan, Scott Meinzen, Sam Lando, and Todd Brandt.

Some plain old cool dudes who I never get to hang out with enough Don Wildman, Jeff Belanger, Andre Snyman, Tont Scire, and Don Lee.

The Springfield Dads of Anarchy-John Ogden, Bruce Stuck, Bruce Loughmiller, Eric Lind, Che Bradley, Alex Layser, Troy Holyrod, Steve Wadsworth, Rob Ittig, Mike Mench, Jimmy Mitchell, Matt Frey, Andy Knoll, Mike Bailey, and Jason Bridges.

This book is especially definitely certainly dedicated to a few men who believed in me and taught me some of the most invaluable lessons on how business, life, and death maybe truly possibly sometimes almost work-Nick Palmisciano (again), Erich Krauss, Steve "Jews Don't Camp" Spiro, Zak "Demon Hunter" Bagans, and James "Rugby is Life" Walker.

Every curmudgeon needs a wingman to tell sordid tales of abuse and lies of grandeur about so a gigantic shout out to the indomitable Greg Sierra who constantly reminds me that it's okay to laugh at life no matter how bad it gets ESPECIALLY when your drunk buddy is puking on the side of the road in the Mojave desert while you run victory laps around him and Military Policemen watch out of sheer amusement.

If I've known or drank with you in my life and your name isn't on this list, don't be offended. I'm old and don't even remember if my penis is supposed to hang to the left or the right during formal events. Because placing your manhood on the wrong side is just tacky.

TABLE OF CONTENTS

INTRODUCTION
LESS CONFORMITY, MORE ANGRY

I heard a guy say "I didn't go to my best friend's funeral because I couldn't deal with it" to which I replied, "You're a pussy." I've always been incensed at the thought of letting my family or friends down in life or in death. A funeral isn't about you or your fragile feelings. It's about respecting the guy who died and comforting his family by showing up and remembering him so all I could think was, "Suck it up, cupcake. You're not the only person who's lost someone."

That's when I knew I was changing. I found myself becoming jaded on people who led a life less challenging and still bitched about it. It wasn't that I hated people, I just disliked being around them and was struggling with a world that demanded I say 'there, there, it's not so bad' when I was really thinking 'quit your whining!'

Learning who you are is not just for teenagers. Men caught up in the very real phenomenon of mid-life panic must rediscover the world around us while also struggling with our own impending mortality and legacy. We usually arrive at 40 carefree, cruising through life with set goals, financial plans, and a steadfast compass, but then nature's tsunami of doubt and anxiety flips the ship and our lives become The Poseidon Adventure. Righting the boat becomes a journey of self-discovery to re-learn much of what we thought we knew. It's natural and somewhat inevitable, so the greatest questions are when will the wave hit? And how big will it be?

As the son of an Army Colonel who was also the son of an Army Colonel, the road I would hoe was never in question and I never felt the need to look inward for answers or share my feelings on the trepidation of stepping out into the real world like a scared puppy. I embraced life after college and reveled in the constantly fluctuating nomadic Army culture for twenty years. I had a plan and was sticking to it with no worries of anything going wrong and nothing did. But then I retired and found myself adrift; lost; confused. I was no longer in the boat, but instead the swimmer frantically trying to tread water while all the other drowning souls clamored over each other, not caring who they pushed under to be saved.

And so was I. In uniform I knew who I was and more importantly I knew where I stood in relation to those around me. It was always right there on my collar and shoulder; a steadfast rank structure that I thrived in, though looking back it's somewhat sad that I needed a uniform to define my life. There's no doubt that it grounded me and taking it off to become a civilian was like learning to walk again and I'd already done that once before after a nasty back injury.

I don't miss the uniform as much as I miss protecting someone (or at least the thought of it). I miss training with soldiers to keep an enemy away from those who were unable to protect themselves. I miss the guys and the mission, but mostly the feeling of being part of a greater good, of being a part of something bigger and more important than myself. Without the Army I was somewhere between the world I knew and the world I didn't want to know. I was Ensign Johnson beaming down to an alien world alongside Captain Kirk, shaky and void of confidence after leaving the security of the mothership. It was only a matter of time until I became the first casualty of the Borg and the audience proclaimed, "saw that one coming, dumbass."

I believe middle-aged men like me are under siege, beset on all sides by personal ambition, internal expectations, familial pressure, disillusionment, uncertainty, and legacy. It's a constant battle to balance the needs of the self and the needs of others and a struggle to discover which ones really take priority. Some win this battle and some tragically lose it.

The Curmudgeon Pressure Cooker

Guys in their sixties and seventies have a clarity on their remaining years that I envy. But what about us forty year-olds who are just getting used to the concept of growing older and, hopefully, wiser? Where do we fit in? Some of us get there and look around and realize we'll never be the best at anything. We haven't achieved all the things we wanted to and will end up in Mediocreville. It's disappointing and for many of us hope fades and with it goes the willingness to fight on. For many this is the midlife crisis trigger.

After going through those years of trying to get ahead and tempering my opinion to fit in and be politically correct in order to minimize confrontation, I got to a point where I just didn't give a damn. I was tired of people trying to make me feel bad for being who I was, so after a while I just didn't give a flying fuck what people thought of me. We live in a world where everyone is offended by everything, but I refuse to change to appease the over-sensitive wussies who keep telling me I'm wrong. This is where I stand and I don't care if you don't like it. If we disagree, then fine. You go your way and I'll go mine. But don't try to make me feel evil or insidious for being me.

We go through life not wanting people to judge us because we want to look cool or seem smart. To be a curmudgeon you have to toss aside your sense of judgment. You can't care if someone thinks you're good, bad, brilliant, stupid, foolish, tacky, or just crapped your pants. There's no feeling of embarrassment or regret or anything, because you don't care what anyone thinks. Judge me and get out of the way.

At some point, you have to embrace your strengths and weaknesses and be comfortable in offending someone. You want to finally feel the blissful liberation of saying what's truly on your mind without considering the consequences. "What are they going to do to me?" becomes your mantra. This is the privilege of age. In a nutshell, it's the recognition that no one can do anything to you that completes the metamorphosis into being a curmudgeon.

Curmudgeonism is not an all-inclusive club. If you're younger or older or even a woman who feels the way we do, then welcome. Pull up your socks, grow a thick skin and don't take anything we say seriously, but let's get something straight right off the bat. I'm not a completely negative "I hate the world" kind of person. I don't bitch about everything and I don't like to associate with people who want to drag you into an abyss of unmitigated hate. But I have an opinion and I'm tired of being told that I can't voice it or that it's wrong. It's an opinion. Don't like it, walk away.

This book is therapy in itself. I left a life of selfless discipline for a life of selfish profiteering and struggled to find myself. It was a traumatic event loaded with unanticipated challenges that definitely triggered a midlife crisis and made me a Level 3 Curmudgeon. I suspect that others go through the same changes so I wanted to reach out and throw them a buoy. Joining the Army was like diving into a raging river that challenges you to cross it. It was all I ever wanted to do; but no one prepared me for getting to the other side. I came out a different person. So where are you in relation to your river? Still swimming it? Reached the other side, tired and shivering and not sure what to do next? Been there. Let me tell you what I've learned from it.

This is NOT a medical diagnosis of middle-aged men nor is it a bullshit psychoanalysis of who they are and what they're going through. It's my own opinion and experience of feeling completely lost as I transitioned into my mid-forties. The current edition of the Oxford English Dictionary defines middle age as "The period of life between young adulthood and old age, now usually regarded as between about forty-five and sixty." That's a wide net to cast, so I whittle it down to the period between when you knew who you were and to the time when you had to relearn it all over again.

The suicide rate among middle aged men in America rose sharply in 2013 especially among men in their 50's. I don't get this and think suicide is selfish and weak (more on that later), so if this book can help out a few of you guys struggling with middle age and contemplating offing yourself, then that's a mission accomplished. This is a guidebook for those suffering a real or imagined midlife crisis or those simply lost in their forties who find themselves saying "I remember when..." way too much. This is for the man who asks, "What am I working so hard for? Why have I missed so much of my life? Is it worth it? And where's the finish line to this absurd race?"

Do you want to lash out but don't know how to and don't want to say something that might dismantle all you've built? Maybe you know how to sound off, but are a little afraid to. Maybe you'll find some inspiration. Maybe you'll think I'm full of shit. Either is fine as long as you take a side. That's lesson number one: don't sit on a fence saying, "well I can see this guy's side of the issues and I can see that guy's side and I'm not sure which one I believe more." Make a decision. I did by writing this book and I damn sure didn't write it to make friends. It's not for everyone, so I invite you to stop reading when you feel offended and then blame your mother for raising a pussy.[1]

As for that guy who couldn't go to his buddy's funeral? I almost became him a few years later. I had a friend who was getting promoted to Colonel and wanted me to be there, but I was hesitant because I wasn't able to achieve the same rank and I knew going to his promotion would only remind me of my own failure. It would suck seeing my friend living my dream life, but I put on a smile and did it anyway. I always had his back and he had mine, so I owed him that. I found the intestinal fortitude to drive on and complete the mission, even making it through Pentagon security with a flask in my pocket. True story.

---

[1] Erin Daniluk

13

WHO IS A CURMUDGEON?

"Curmudgeons are mockers and debunkers whose bitterness is a symptom rather than a disease. They can't compromise their standards and can't manage the suspension of disbelief necessary for feigned cheerfulness. They're constantly ticked off because they're constantly aware of so much to be ticked off about."

-Jon Winokur

The modern curmudgeon is much less the WWII vet yelling "get off my lawn!" than it is Gran Torino's Walt Kowalski who uses hate and cunning to construct a grand scheme that ultimately fucks you forever. We're vindictive and forged by a variety of variables and life events that were both tragic and joyous. On the whole we're disappointed in our fellow man and don't have much hope for mankind. We're disillusioned on those hopeful adolescent lessons about how the world ought to look because we've felt firsthand the way it does look and it's made us jaded and overly honest. If you're an idiot then we're not only going to tell you so, but feel it's our duty to do so.

The metamorphosis into curmudgeonism consists of several phases of trying to find out where we fit into the grand scheme of things. It starts with doubt and anxiety before passing into full-fledged panic that leads to self-discovery and realization before finally blossoming as a beautiful acceptance of how flawed life really is when we utter the immortal curmudgeon philosophy, "fuck it!" At that moment we're reborn into the same world, but as more confident and less apologetic men with a higher level of clarity and lower level of tolerance. We've hacked our way through the jungle of life only to come upon the swift river of midlife. We know we have to dive in and swim across but who will emerge on the far shore? The chances of it being the same person are slim.

Though way overused Henry David Thoreau famously said, "The mass of men lead lives of quiet desperation," which hints at who curmudgeons really are. Some say this quote is about misplaced value at how we feel a void in our lives and attempt to fill it with things that make us feel better about ourselves. That may have been true of Thoreau's time, but in the 21st century it's apropos for men who just want to be who they are inside but can't find the courage to do just that. We're so ingrained in the notion of doing and saying what is acceptable in society that we frequently squash the inner self and create a persona that we're told is better than who we are at our base.

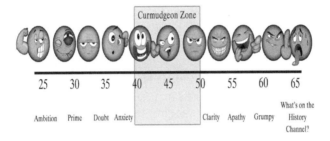

The Curmudgeon Zone

A curmudgeon is not a grump, grouch, snob, or dick, which confuses the life out of people when you tell them there's actually a difference. A curmudgeon may evolve into one of those eventually (pour out a drop of bourbon for my lost homies), but we're not the completely irascible types who are mean for no reason. There's always a meaning to our bitterness and therefore a fine line between curmudgeons and complete sadomasochistic assholes. The latter harbor irreparably damaged souls that curmudgeons actually fear turning into. They're social pariahs with terminal frustration and anger that can't be helped nor do they want to be. They're to be avoided at all costs lest they drag you down into their world of shit.

A curmudgeon is not a critic per se, but a holds a very wary stink eye towards people in general and is more savvy than an Arab trader.[2] Food critics, movie critics, and book critics are all smug, pretentious souls doomed to a depressing life void of pleasure and are most certainly not curmudgeons. A critic is so ensconced in the memories of the mountaintop that they're blind to the beauties of the valley below and their unrealistic standards make it impossible for them to ever feel satisfaction. They live in a constant world of disappointment where the only pleasure is in mocking that which they don't like and questioning what they don't understand. They view the world as being full of Quislings who need their divine intervention lest they ruin it for the rest of their kind. Sorry...got caught up in my hate again. It won't be the last time.

Curmudgeons are selectively optimistic. We believe in the promising outlook for our own lives, but not the world in general. Once a man gets to a comfortable place mentally, he doesn't let the little things get him down and doesn't buy into anyone's whining and complaining about inconsequential crap. We've realized (or are about to) that there is a much bigger picture in life than the 50-meter target, and reaching level 80 on Candy Crush means less than ball sweat in the grand scheme of things. On a scale from dirt to supernova there are a lot more important things in life than Miley Cyrus taking her clothes off, so we don't get our panties in a bunch worrying over silly stuff like whether or not Hannah Montana is a good role model. She's not. End of story.

We have a solid perspective on the way the world works versus the way it should work and still hold out hope

---

[2] A Christmas Story callout. Curmudgeons don't even need to read this silly footnote because they recognize it immediately.

(though a slim one) that it will impress us someday. This is important. Go back and read that sentence again. We're pissed because we know how much there is to be pissed at. What it boils down to is curmudgeonism = clarity, but that doesn't mean we're arrogant (unless we're dealing with lazy Occupy Wall Street hippies). We've divorced ourselves from caring what anyone else thinks. We still enjoy discourse, but in the end it's unlikely we'll be swayed by anything anyone says so a more accurate term would be 'belligerent.'

Curmudgeonism is a heavy boot on the throat of ignorance and is best expressed through body language and tone of voice. It's not just what you say, but how you say it. We simply don't have the time or tolerance for the idiots of society; a demographic that seems to be growing exponentially since the turn of the century. We like to say things in a way that makes the receiver of the statement either feel bad for being ignorant or feel small for being stupid (as long as it's deserved). A surly tone of voice dripping with contempt is a dead giveaway of a curmudgeon, which is why information technology makes it harder to spot us on that infernal interweb thing.

For example, if someone emails you "I'm going to the market," you can't tell if it's a simple courtesy or an accusation. It could be an innocent statement like, "Hey friend. I'm going to the market if you need anything" or it could be an accusation, as in "I'm going to the market because you're too damn lazy to do it yourself!" Curmudgeons don't like ambiguity. We want you to know without a shadow of a doubt when we're saying something that you should take as offensive so emails and text messaging rob us of that ability.

Curmudgeons get squirrely in the middle of their lives but ultimately embrace it after a healthy dose of therapy (therapy = booze) and while it may sound like we hate everything, that's not usually true. It's all about clarity, perspective, and confidence. We're Obiwan Kenobis who have learned a smattering of the ways of the universe and know that looking backward at what's gone is not as important as looking forward to what will be. We've figured out a golden rule – freaking out about the fact that your life is halfway over is not as important as making the second half something to be proud of.

Not all men arrive at curmudgeonism through a midlife crisis though many of us get there because of it. Some are naturally gifted at being cantankerous, but they're usually not the right type of person to be a curmudgeon. Don't think there's a difference? Is there a difference between an Alabama redneck and a Kansas redneck? Damn skippy there is. You have to get jaded on life to become a curmudgeon, which usually involves a great personal loss of some type that causes you to lose faith in humanity and throw aside the drudges of societal norms. That usually excludes men in their thirties because, like the Vice President, they're just not quite there yet. They can be crabby, plain-spoken, or bitchy, but they lack the real life experiences and attitude to be true curmudgeons and in fact, frequently ridicule us for being the way we are. Blame the internet.

Curmudgeons have stopped trying to convince people that they're right. I don't care about your views or whether not they are in line with mine. If I don't agree with you then I just say to myself "you're an idiot" and walk away. You're going to have a hard life living with your stupid opinions but you know what? Hopefully the incessant nagging from others and constantly having to defend yourself will make you stronger in the long run or at least see the light that you're wrong. Or you will just die. Either way I don't care.

STAGE 1 CURMUDGEONS

"Shall I after tea and cakes and ices,
Have the strength to force the moment to its crisis?
I have seen the moment of my greatness flicker,
I have seen the eternal footman hold my coat and snicker,
And in short I was afraid"
-TS Eliot

It's almost difficult to call these people curmudgeons in the strict sense of the word because they're still confused about life and have a long way to go before embracing their "I don't give a shit" side yet. They're really curmudgeon larvae who will eventually transform into hardened, confident, unflinching crab pots someday. Stage 1's are in the WTF Zone and have a hard time figuring out where they fit in life. Their life compass is spinning out of control while their disciplined and organized brains scream for a roadmap. Level 1's are starting to realize a few things:

-They don't like to be touched, so keep your grubby mitts off.

-They hate inefficient people. A person who takes just as much time to pass off a task as it would have taken them to do it themselves is a douche.

-They are growing increasingly intolerant of people who don't follow basic logic and rules. Someone spent many months engineering the blinkers on your car. Use them.

-They will reuse an item well past its life expectancy.

-They hate to waste time without a return on the investment because they're realizing they don't have many years left and have to maximize them. If there isn't a payoff to a hallway conversation then get lost. As a side effect, Stage 1 Curmudgeons are not only punctual but will hold anyone late for a meeting in eternal contempt for wasting their time.

-They hate to listen to a story that has no point or punch line. If you're going to take ten minutes of my life to tell me about a fishing trip then it better end with you noodling out a 50 pounder with your penis or it's just not worth it. And for God's sake don't try to tell a story to be funny or accepted that just makes you look stupid. "So when I was rushing my frat in college we had to crawl around on our hands and knees like elephants and stick our finger up the ass of the guy in front of us. You should have seen it." No...I shouldn't have.

-They hate contrived reality TV shows and unrealistic movies.

-They refuse to use shorthand to type text messages. "R U going 2 th partee 2-nite" is not in a curmudgeon's lexicon. However...

-They use short answers in person because they don't care enough about someone to explain themselves.
Example:
Did you see the fights last night?
Yes.
What did you think?
Awesome.
Can anyone beat Fighter X?
No.
Cool. Well then, um...doing anything this weekend?
My wife.

-They scoff when they hear anyone under 30 use the term "my whole entire life" as in, "I've been waiting for this moment my whole entire life." Your whole entire life consists of a blip on my radar, jackhole.

-They find themselves wanting to apologize for past grievances when they were young and stupid. *Example:* An old girlfriend finds a curmudgeon on Facebook and berates him for being a dick to her in college. All he says is "You're right. I was a douchebag then and treated you pretty badly." Around this time Level 1's watch a lot of Ally McBeal.

They're becoming increasingly intolerant of people who can't make a decision. "Well...I don't know" doesn't benefit anyone. A Stage 1 Curmudgeon looks at the indecisive and thinks, "grab your gonads, roll chicken bones, consult a Ouija board, do whatever you have to do to get rid of your spineless jellyfish syndrome and make a decision! I'll respect you more if you do, even if it's totally wrong."[3]

STAGE 2 CURMUDGEONS
"I only go out to get me a fresh appetite for being alone."
-Lord Byron

The Stage 2 Curmudgeon is in the golden zone. He's tired of apologizing for who he is, doesn't want to compromise anymore, and doesn't want to let the world make him feel badly for his beliefs. This is the core of

---

[3] Not entirely true. If someone picks the wrong course of action after being warned not to, then it's acceptable to cup your hands over your mouth and shout "I TOLD YOU SO!"

21

Curmudgeonism and it's taking root in the man during stage 2. A Stage 2 Curmudgeon...

-Doesn't feel like he's owed anything and is quick to remind you that you aren't owed anything either. Want a new Xbox? Go mow some lawns, kid.

-Swears more frequently. Get the fuck over it.

-Responds to questions with frightfully obvious answers.
Example:
"How are we going to win this game?"
"Score more points."

-Points out the obvious, even If it's painful for someone in the room, albeit with slight reservation. He still tempers his comments to a degree, but only if it means his wife or girlfriend will withhold sex or his comments will make their way back to the wife or girlfriend who will react by withholding sex. Otherwise all bets are off.

-Can't stand those who hurt women and/or kids. They're fucking scum. It SHOULD be a characteristic of the human race, but we all know it's not. If anything riles up a Stage 2 Curmudgeon to resort to fisticuffs it's this. Slap a chick in a bar and I'll throw a chair at you like Geraldo. However, he also...

-Knows kids have to learn, even if that means getting hurt doing something stupid. Some kids learn through books. Others through sticking their finger in the fire twice just to make sure that it really is hot. It's just a law of the universe and going against it is bad juju.

-Is getting craftier in his ways and is starting to realize that the "fuck you asshole" reaction is not nearly as satisfying as a complicated scheme to get a douchebag fired.

-Doesn't like to be the center of attention. He's a little more withdrawn and prefers to be the man behind the man...especially Caligula.

-Doesn't want anyone's help. He'll do it all himself because that's the only way to ensure the job is done right.

-Questions why before taking a risk. As a youth he didn't mind it and even sought it out on occasion. Now there has to be a payoff. Stage 2 Curmudgeons don't jump out of a plane for the same old rush that they experienced years ago. There has to be something more to it. There has to be a higher meaning for taking the risk; like riding a bull raises a kajillion dollars for a dying kid. Without the return on the investment, risky behavior is less appealing and increasingly unnecessary.

-Doesn't want to show weakness in public. Stage 2's still struggle with the manly side that tells them not to get teary while the patriotic/familial side tells them it's okay. There are some moments in a man's life when he wants to get misty and he's still trying to figure out what those are. Funerals, a daughter's wedding, and the national anthem are okay. Oprah reruns are not.

-Laughs at anyone who makes the same mistake twice. If you can't learn from slamming your dick in a car door then there's just no hope for you.

-Is tired of being told he has to be open-minded. There are some things you can't convince a curmudgeon of because he's spent a lifetime not only learning the lesson through books, but living it through practical experience. He's not going to be swayed on certain issues and has no inclination to discuss them, so when someone says "You need to be more open minded about X," the curmudgeon takes on the role of Infidel and says "No, I don't have to be open-minded about something that I'm unwilling to change my views on and you're an idiot for thinking the way you do. Thor is good and Loki is evil. No matter how many times you show me a fleeting moment of him being genuine in comic books, he's still evil to the core!"

-Doesn't over-think things. Some people try WAY too hard to find a solution to a problem, come up with a successful course of action, or just describe an object.
Example:
Beer Critic: "This is a full bodied beer with flavor, balance, and complexity. It has hints of spice and fruit and sweetness that awaken your palette and leave you reminiscing of youthful days when your faithful Golden Retriever frolicked in the snow while you sat comfortably by a fire. If he drank alcohol, the Dalai Lama would proclaim it holy."
Curmudgeon: "Really? Cause it just tastes like fucking beer to me, douchebag."

-Doesn't quote music lyrics as life lessons and view singers who use "yeah" and "whoa" as uncreative.

-Doesn't worship entertainers. Kids have the luxury of idolizing entertainers because they don't know any better. Adults do. Curmudgeons know that a guy on a stage is there because we paid him to sing and dance and entertain us. Remember these are people who name their kids North, River, and Apple. Watch their movies and walk away, but...

-Stage 2 Curmudgeons realize they need to feel a story instead of just hear it. They don't want people to tell them what happened, but say it in a way that makes them interested. Bring us into the world you describe with prose and savvy. Don't just tell us about New York, take me to Soho, Tribeca, or the Carnegie Deli and bring a steaming pile of sensuous corned beef into our lives. Show me the nuances of your city and make me want to go there.

-Doesn't believe men should have elective, cosmetic plastic surgery unless it's to repair something innately necessary like a face disfigured by combat. Nose jobs and eyelifts for vanity's sake scream out insecurity and curmudgeons don't let insecure people into the inner circle. Female breast augmentation is totally cool though.

-Embraces useful change and scoffs at silly uses of technology. Farmville, Angry Birds, and Foursquare? No thanks. An app that shows where my kids and my bourbon are at all times? Sign me up.

-Looks people in the eye when they speak and demands the same in return. It's just common courtesy and if you can't look at someone when you speak then what makes you think they can believe anything you say?

-Makes the worst tour guide.

-Hates paper cuts. They really, really sting.[4]

---

[4] Nick Palmisciano, CEO of Ranger Up

STAGE 3 CURMUDGEONS
"I can unload my opinion on anyone at anytime."
-Anthony Bourdain

Stage 3 Curmudgeons are exiting the golden zone and finding out who they really are, which can fall between the ages of 45 and 50, but everyone is different. Curmudgeonism is event-driven, not time-driven meaning it all depends on who you are and where you are in life. Just because one lucky guy reached stage 3 at age 45 doesn't mean you will too.

Stage 3 is a glorious time because the curmudgeon's self-realization is taking over and his intolerance for morons, weasels, and pindicks has set in. He's hardened and unencumbered by societal norms, so he speaks his mind no matter what the consequence to the horror of every birthday party, pool social, Faceboook friend, and Boy Scout meeting.

Stage 3 Curmudgeons are finding a piece of intellectual real estate to plant their flag and say "This is me. This is where I stand. I would be happier if you agreed with me, but if you don't, stay away and leave me be. I don't have the time or inclination to argue with you."

In general, Stage 3 Curmudgeons:

-Love to remind you that things were tough when we were your age. Because they were god dammit! You have no idea how easy you have it, kid.

-Are brutally honest and don't care if it hurts. At this level we REALLY don't care what people think just like I won't care if you dislike this book. It's all about not apologizing for who you are. That doesn't mean being a dick, but it does mean taking a stand for what you believe in and not backing down. Stage 3's are confident in themselves and their actions. You are who you are and that's not going to change. In this stage we frequently revert back to when we were kids and had no filters on our mouths. "You're a boogerface" is now "you're a galactic dumbass."

-Cannot be swayed on core beliefs. There are some things you cannot convince me are good for anyone. Welfare? Stupid. Socialism? How'd that work out for anyone who's tried it? In battle with the US Army, some Native American tribes would tie themselves to the ground so they couldn't run. That's right, they tied a fucking rope from their neck to a spike in the ground so no matter how intense the fight got it was physically impossible for them to leave the field of battle. Being a Stage 3 Curmudgeon is absolutely nothing like swinging a hatchet with a leash around your throat, but standing your ground no matter how bad things get is a core ethic in this stage of life, so it's somewhat remotely comparable and makes total sense after a few cocktails.

-Are set in our ways and have earned the right to be unmovable and opinionated. Our stance on life doesn't come from books and theories, but practical experience and time. In stage 3 we're realizing exactly who we are and liberating the internal ambition to pursue what we want.

-Will kill or die for family and friends. If you're in the inner circle of friends then a curmudgeon has your back with extreme prejudice. We need someone or something to protect and hold dear. This could be anything from a wife and kids to a house to a favorite car to a voodoo doll acquired on a New Orleans bender that involved Leo DiCaprio defiling a willow tree. Doesn't matter what it is, but at the heart of every curmudgeon is an object or person that anchors him and has to be meticulously cared for and protected or he doesn't have meaning in his life and therefore no reason to be curmudgeonly. It's like being in the military. If you don't understand then I can't explain it to you, but here's a picture that might help.

The Curmudgeon Universe

-Increasingly hate the way people treat people. Stories of bullying, rape, torture, murder, and abominable behavior incense us more and more. Stage 3 Curmudgeons find themselves wanting to stick up for the weak and finding the courage to do so.

-Respect hard work and hate laziness. Curmudgeons have an especially uncomfortable place in their heart for those who don't try and just mooch off of those who do. Intelligent people who don't apply their potential or just get by without making an effort and have no work ethic are diametrically opposed to the curmudgeon and deserve a festering genital rash.

-Don't compromise their principles. We don't change who we are when we learn that the dude we've been having drinks with for hours is really powerful and rich. He's still just a dude having drinks.

-Aren't impressed with anyone's "great idea." We've seen it before and know a Dyson loses suction, Ginsu knives get dull, and there is no wonder drug in the entire world that keeps a boner up for more than a few minutes.

-Understand the value of tangible and intangible things and gets his money's worth. Curmudgeons drive a hard bargain, rarely give anything away, and can't be sold on anything. We say "I'm not paying for that" frequently, so keep walking all you carpet baggers.

-Don't jump to conclusions and know there are two sides to every story. It's naïve to believe everything you hear and at this stage we don't trust many because we've seen people who will lie, cheat, and manipulate others to get their way.

-Live and let live. A lot of the characteristics of curmudgeons combine here. We're not interested in arguing with people who are at the opposite end of the spectrum from us because we don't care about them enough to. We're set in our ways and don't feel the need to debate that which we already know to be true. Some curmudgeons have experienced firsthand the debilitating heartache of a life lost too soon or some other form of loss and know that sweating the little things is a waste of time (unless life, limb, eyesight, teeth or reputation are involved then we get pissy about attention to detail). If you want to be an idiot then go do it outside my sphere of influence.

-Say something that starts a heated debate and then walk away when we're bored because we know we're right and don't care how it turns out. Take this book for example.

-Start conversations with "I don't give a shit about..." We like to make it known that what's important to you is not important to us.
Example:
A printer says, "We accidentally printed 246 more books than you asked for, so we have to charge you $700 more." Curmudgeon reply - "I don't give a shit about your inability to count. I'm not paying for it."

-End conversations with "got it." When you're young and you disagree with someone you make it known by getting in their face and vehemently arguing your position and ending it with "you're an idiot!" Curmudgeons just stop listening, wait for their opponent to finish, say "got it," and walk away.

-Vent out loud when no one is looking. Some people dance in front of the mirror, we bitch at it. Even when someone catches us, we continue to bitch to the air, the walls and the carpet because we don't like leaving our thoughts dangling and they just keep staring at us judgingly. If we're going to take the time to vent then we're going to get it all out.

-Aren't afraid to make crude jokes at their spouse in private.
Example:
Wife – Can you take out some sausage?
Curmudgeon – Right here? Well, okay.
Wife – From the freezer!

-Stay as far away as possible from only one subject: religion. To each his own on this one. The one possible exception is the disdain we have for athletes who thank God for their successes instead of crediting their own physical abilities. Cause if there is a God, he doesn't get involved in sporting events and does not help anyone score a touchdown. You did that on your own, champ.

-Don't really pine for being young again because they know they were idiots. The privileges of youth are nothing compared to the privileges of age.

-Have more refined palates and are more selective about food. Spaghetti-O's and Pop Tarts were great when we were young, but we don't have enough time left in our lives to eat Ramen or Chicken of the Sea.

-Have a sense of humor, but it sometimes comes at someone else's expense. Curmudgeons are sarcastic, but not in a 'I want to drag you into my dark world of pain" way. Stage 3's seek out the comedians of life and avoid the true haters of it.

-Never say 'just joking' even when they are.

-Don't believe in suicide. It's selfish and weak.

CURMUDGEON MAXIMS

Absolutes and stereotypes debase the person or persons being profiled, but it's an undeniable fact that there are patterns and trends among certain peoples. When thousands or even millions of humans have generally the same mindset they get labeled (which immediately causes many of them to deny that label out of fear of conformity). While all of us are different, there are some core curmudgeon beliefs that pervade the massive crowd of middle-aged men in the world.

This section may seem a little disjointed, but it's presented in short soundbytes for a few reasons:

1) To get to the point without a lot of fluff.

2) To provide you with short phrases that you can use as ammunition in your lives when you encounter someone who needs curmudgeonly advice or just a verbal thrashing.

3) To let you pick and choose what you agree or disagree with and develop your own curmudgeonly basis.

You should read this section with a Sharpie so you can put a star next to the passages you like and a big fat black line through the ones you don't.

YOUTH
"You don't have bad luck. Bad things happen to you because you're a dumbass."
-Red Forman

I overheard a 40-year old man say, "I wish I was young again." Why? We were idiots wrapped in a cocoon of stupid and only survived through blind luck. We were broke, in and out of relationships, and didn't know jack about the way the world worked. There are advantages to being long in the tooth that you don't realize until you get there. Youth is like The Congo. It's nice to visit, but there's no reason to live there again.

We all get nostalgic about how great it would be to be young again, but why pine for the days of not being able to handle your liquor and anxiously awaiting that first sexual experience? How was it cool that we were poor and didn't know how to drive? Even in college when I could do, drink, and fuck anything I wanted to, it wasn't nirvana because I didn't know it at the time. I thought it would last forever and didn't realize how fleeting the experience was so I didn't value it. I had no idea how free and fun my surroundings were until I left them and looked back years later wondering where they went.

I was a young twenty something stationed in Korea, unable to speak the language, unknowing of anything but the beaten path that westerners walked, unaware of the beauties of their culture. So to make up for it, my fellow rapscallion Lieutenants and I drank and chased skirts all the while counting down the days of returning to the land of the Big Mac. We had camaraderie, we had cheap beer, we had the privilege of leading troops against an enemy just 30 clicks away, and we had all the makings of epic stories. Yet we were ignorant twenty-something's who couldn't see past our beer mugs and didn't realize until much later that it was one of the greatest years of our lives. If you're in heaven and don't know it, then what good is it?

Sure there are unforgettable moments while growing up, but they're unrepeatable and for good reason. The first time a motor vehicle moved forward with you at the controls. The first time you got into a fistfight and realized you'd conquered your fears and the stinging in your face was temporary and totally worth it. The first time you saw a proud parent looking down at you from the stands of your high school basketball game as you scored a jump shot. The mind-blowing feeling of your first orgasm. These things are irreplaceable, but they're over now and not coming back. Quit holding onto the past and get over it.

Life as a kid is not better than life as an adult. Some think their fading memories of what was once great are superior to what they have now. They always mourn the past and talk about how simpler things were then. They're stuck at the zenith of their lives and unable to let go of it. They pick the happiest times and live like they're still there, waxing poetic about how great it was.

That's sad.

Look forward, not back and when you lose sight of who you are break out the night vision goggles. And by night vision goggles I mean bourbon.

Watching younger men and women in their physical prime is absolutely excruciating when you're injured or starting to feel the effects of age. They run, cut left and right, pass a ball, jump, say 'bro' a lot, and hula hoop circles around us while we grab our knees, wheeze, and pop Motrin like they're Skittles.

It's like being a prisoner in Alcatraz (I imagine) watching the carefree youth making the most of their lives across the bay in San Francisco. We're trapped. Not necessarily incarcerated, but still a prisoner of our own bodies...limited to only playing at half the level of everyone else. In our day we were just as nimble as they are now, but they're the masters of this world. Our character and bank accounts may be astronomically larger, but their knees and back don't buckle from the strain of carrying a kid or a wallet that has more than a free taco coupon in it. If there's anywhere that envy rears its ugly head and whispers malevolence in the curmudgeon's ear, it's here. Young men shouldn't play golf. It should be reserved for those of us avoiding muscle atrophy late in life. Play risky games while you can...bro.

A big reason curmudgeons are surly is because we look at the youth of today and only see a bunch of dumbasses who will probably ruin everything we worked so hard for. After decades of toil and personal sacrifice to make the world better a better place all we see are a group of idiots who will undo it all without a second thought. How depressing.

But then again being young is all about being ignorant. Young people still don't realize how vicious life is and how horrible people can be, so we comfort ourselves by remembering that this precious young person is still an idiot. He lives life to the fullest because he just doesn't know any better. Having fun is all he's really had to care about. He has the luxury of a roof over his head and hot meals on the table. He doesn't have to hunt and gather for himself or make money to get by, so life is fairly easy. When he gets into the real world it's suddenly "fend for yourself" and things get scary. Here's looking at you, kid.

FEAR

"Bite on the bullet old man, and don't let them think you're afraid."

-Rudyard Kipling

Fear is a tricky thing in middle age because it grows within us in some ways and dies in others. Fear is a critical part of our lives that has to be understood and managed. As we get into midlife, we don't want to take risks like we used to, but at the same time we're finding the courage to say the things we always wanted to. Jump out of an airplane? No thanks. Tell an idiot he's out in left field trying to score a touchdown with a hockey puck? Absolutely. The things that scare younger people don't scare us and vice versa. Horror movies aren't scary. Real life is. At least that's what TV shows like Gang Wars are banking on.

Fear is derived from knowing the risks involved with a certain act. As children we don't fear flying because we don't know that planes are made by men prone to mistakes and have never seen one fall out of the sky. As teenagers we don't fear driving because we've never seen the splayed out bodies of other teens on a road that results from a high-speed crash (in a conflict between flesh and metal, metal wins). As adults we learn to fear because we know what cause and effect is. So fear first and foremost derives from the knowledge of the potential consequences of an action.

The second source of fear is self-preservation. To fear death, I have to have a sincere passion for living, otherwise I don't care if I die and therefore don't fear it. To fear a fistfight I have to know about superficial and internal pain and have to care enough about my personal health to either avoid it or make sure I win. To fear a verbal confrontation I have to know the immense emotional and spiritual pain it brings to lose one. If you respect someone you may fear arguing with him because if you lose he won't respect you back and that sucks so you do everything you can to win. Humans like to win because when we win, nothing hurts. It's the need to avoid embarrassment, bodily harm, or death and the desire to preserve oneself that truly drives fear.

But that's where courage kicks in because there can be no courage without fear. Curmudgeons believe the risk of telling the truth is not only worthwhile but necessary in a world that revolves around inflated self-interest and delusional expectations, so we find the courage to overcome fear and give the world what it needs: a healthy dose of honesty. But you have to have the stones to do that, so reach down and make sure those huevos have a thick skin. Sack up.

COURAGE

"I have several times made a poor choice by avoiding a necessary confrontation."

-John Cleese

As much as Curmudgeonism is a state of mind, it is equally a state of action. We're honest and don't sugar coat anything so we actually make the world better by pointing out the things others won't. It's our moral imperative and lot in life, but it takes courage. It's not easy to tell someone they're wrong and doing so tends to rub some people the wrong way. We're like a suppository of constructive criticism-itchy and invasive, but ultimately therapeutic. In the end we help the individual being critiqued, so it's a worthwhile cause. Otherwise the moron in question will continue to think he's Galacticus when at best he's Ant Man. Courage is a ventricle in the dark, throbbing heart of Curmudgeonism that feeds the blood it needs to keep pumping.

An example everyone can relate to is Simon Cowell. He'll kill your dreams before they get off the ground and although his delivery is somewhat harsh, he saves people a lot of time they would otherwise waste pursuing an untenable goal. He's a curmudgeon's hero who has the courage to be honest and the apathy to back it up.

Let's say you're in a meeting and someone says, "I have an idea...we need to hold a testicle licking contest for morale" and everyone agrees. Have the moral courage to point out the ludicrousness of the idea before it actually takes root. If you don't protest the group consensus and refuse to taste sweaty balls, then you're two things: weak and weird. There's nothing wrong with being weird, but being weak is inexcusable. If you're present when a bad decision is made, then you're not part of the solution, but part of the problem. You can't be a mousy, quiet guy (or gal) who lets others walk off a cliff without stopping them.

This is especially true when it comes to bosses. It's an employee's duty tell his boss when he's fucked up. I once had a boss who was allergic to being on time and would make everyone wait for him well past the start time of every meeting. One day after being 30 minutes late I pulled homeboy aside and told him how he was wasting an average of 10 man hours a week by making everyone wait for him instead of working. Telling your boss he's wrong is always never fun and I expected a Bloods versus Crips throwdown, but I was also right and he knew it. In the end nothing changed and I learned that some people go right back to their bad habits (think Kirstie Alley and Weight Watchers), but at least I had the courage to do the right thing.

Some mistake brutal honesty with meanness, which is terminological inexactitude.[5] We like to voice our opinion on how we see the world and that usually comes across in an un-politically correct way, but we're not mean. Abrasive, yes, but remember we're jaded and don't care if someone's tail feathers get a little ruffled. The best way to deal with us is to stand your ground. If a curmudgeon challenges your manhood and you bend like a prison whore for a pack of smokes then he will continue to berate you. But if you say "Hell yeah I drive a Prius with PSSYCAT on the license plate!" then good on you. We respect the courage it takes to believe in who you are no matter whether we agree with it or not.

---

[5] Shout out to one of the greatest curmudgeons ever, Sir Winston Churchill

DECISIVENESS
"In too much of the West, everyone wants the guarantee of safety and never having to make any decisions."
-Anthony Bourdain

Indecisiveness is so unattractive. The inability to make a decision and then have the moral courage to see it through is a quality that sets a relationship on its head for curmudgeons. "Well I don't know...what do you want to do?" is like kicking us in the nuts. We double over not from anguish, but from the realization that we wasted time hanging around a wet noodle and there are still people in the world who are born without a spine.

We want people to weigh their options, pick a course of action, and support it with confidence. A great leader is someone who's confident in himself and his ability to recognize a situation and make a sound decision. Middle age brings experience to the table and the realization that we have learned one great truth of this world-there isn't enough time left in our lives to pussyfoot around and wait until tomorrow to act.

Making a decision is a difficult thing for those without conviction. It could be as mundane as choosing between cereal and eggs for breakfast or as monumental as dropping an A-Bomb on Japan, but whatever the outcome, pick a path and walk it with your head held high. Choosing not to make a decision is sometimes a viable option, but not really because it's hard to stick with inaction; and letting someone else decide by proxy leaves your fate in the hands of others. Who wants that?

Middle-agers have realized that a big part of defining our life lies in the choices we have to make with the best available information at our disposal. Go to college or go to work? Get married or stay single? Have kids or start a virtual farm? Stack cups or play a sport that requires you to wear one? Every decision opens one door and closes the opposing door, usually permanently. To oversimplify it, life is like a tree. For the first part of our lives, we all do the same thing-go to school. This is the trunk.

Then as we go on through life we choose one branch and go down it until a crossroads presents us with another decision. Which branch do you choose? The cycle repeats itself over and over again until we find ourselves on the end of a branch as a leaf waiting to fall back to the ground to decompose and be reclaimed by the earth. What part of the tree you end up in is in your hands. It could be high up basking in the sunlight, lost in the middle of the crowd, or on the low branches, decrepit and alone. Choose wisely.

DISCRETION

"The great Chinese classics have always said that it's better not to fight; that the clever man achieves his ends without violence; that a battle delayed is better than a battle fought."
-John Keegan

If you're gonna lock horns, make sure you have a big rack because the last thing any curmudgeon wants is to pitch into a fight only to find himself decisively engaged over a topic he really doesn't care that much about. This is the fine line between decisiveness and discretion and it creates a moral dilemma because we love to speak our minds, but some things just aren't worth going to the mat over. Knowing when it's best to walk away and let someone win or think they've won (which can be great leverage in some relationships) is difficult. By middle age we're figuring out what we're willing to get into a dance off for and what can be sacrificed for a better endstate.

There's a saying: "Better to be silent and thought the fool than to open your mouth and remove all doubt."

This may have been true when we were young and cared about looking stupid, but curmudgeons don't give a fat rat's ass if someone thinks us a fool. Many times in my youth I wish I'd kept my mouth shut, but only because I truly had no idea what I was talking about and said something dumb like "farts smell good." With age comes experience and (hopefully) a sense of wisdom that makes much of what we say grounded in real world truth.

Two types of people it does no good to ever argue with are referees and cops. Have you ever seen a professional referee change his mind when a player argues with him? Has an umpire ever said, "You know what...you're right. That probably wasn't a strike. Ball three. And next time please don't mention my mother's virtue." Have you ever gotten out of a ticket by starting a fight with a police officer? If so kudos for you, but oftentimes the opposite outcome is more likely. "Go fuck yourself pig" only results in being hogtied (ironically), taken to jail, and being ridiculed on TheSmokingGun.com. With refs and cops, discretion is a rule, but other times fighting is not only alright, it's goddamn necessary.

Example:

You and two friends go out on the town one Saturday night. Friend A (drunk) insists on driving Friend B (drunk) and Friend C (drunk) home. When Friend A refuses to give up the keys to his bitchin' Camaro, Friend B knocks him clean out, tosses C the keys and says, "Call us a cab, bro." The potential for loss of life, limb, eyesight, and reputation are all good reasons to stand your ground and throw a verbal barrage or dust off the soupbones and mix it up no matter whose feelings it hurts.

Curmudgeon quiz

A co-worker walks past you and you notice he's not wearing a tie in the office when the company dress code clearly states he should. Do you:

a. Say "Where's your ugly tie, Dave?"
b. Say "Guess I'll just take these pants off since CLEARLY there's no reason to follow the dress code around here!"
c. Wait for him to get upset with you for something and throw it back at the most opportune time for maximum embarrassment.

This is a trick question. Depending on the work relationship (boss vs non-boss) and personal relationship (the guy's a dick or not), the curmudgeon generally picks option B or C. Option A is a sure way to start a fight and though we don't mind confrontation, an unnecessary provocation is not the optimal outcome unless there's a clear benefit (like he's a dick and his boss is within earshot, in which case FIRE IN THE HOLE!).

You have to pick your battles and failing to adhere to a dress code usually isn't a reason to launch Hellfire missiles, though it depends on your situation. Some will tell you it's a perfect reason to start a fight because we all have to have standards, no matter how inconsequential they might seem. The discreet man will put this event in his pocket and save it for later.

Picking your battles is closely related to the 'live and let live' philosophy that is a running theme of curmudgeonism. It's sometimes better to walk away and let stupid be stupid than waste your precious life energy trying to fix it. Most people think curmudgeons are intolerant, but I say we're more tolerant than most because we have to have a good reason to engage.
Example:

In Korea there's no concept of "personal space." It's such a crowded country that there's no room for your little aura. Subways are jammed packed and the prevailing joke is "How many Koreans can you get on a subway? One more." That concept translates over to the road where a driver with a one-inch advantage over the other can change lanes and come as close as he wants to hitting you and you're not supposed to get mad.

Now let's take that concept over the ocean to the USA. You cut a guy off in traffic and you could get your ass shot off. But if it's a Korean guy cutting you off then it's not really his fault. It's his culture's. It's all he's known growing up. Let it go.

It's the same with my local burger joint. Ricardo is from Rio de Janeiro and has absolutely no concept of urgency. Where he's from no one is in a hurry. It's a laid back culture where the one o'clock jiu jitsu class always starts at two so I get used to being served at a leisurely pace because he doesn't know any other way. There's no point getting bitchy with Ricardo because it won't do any good. He doesn't think the way we do and never will, so I let it go.

Beware people who don't know the meaning of "live to fight another day." Nothing is more dangerous than a friend without discretion; even a prudent enemy is preferable.[6]

---

[6] Jean de La Fontaine

PROFESSIONALISM
"He's a gentleman. He still feels guilty when his wife sucks his dick."

-Me, drunk

At this point you might get the impression that a curmudgeon is always rude and crude. Not at all true. We have no problem being professional, which means taking emotion out of the equation and saying or doing the right thing even if we disagree with it. When others let anger, fear, sadness, frustration, whatever take over their lives, the professional man stays calm and lets experience be his guide. As we get older, restraint and tolerance shrink and we let our emotions get the best of us because we give less of a shit who we offend. Middle-aged men (especially Stage 1 Curmudgeons) struggle with the things we think versus the things we actually say and have a harder time being professional, but that doesn't mean we can't.

Example:
Someone approaches you in the hallway at work and you can tell he wants to talk, but you don't want to. "Good morning Bob," he says. "How are you today?" An awkward response like "Horny!" would shut him down and accomplish the desired outcome of getting rid of him, but if you would never say that then you're a curmudgeon struggling with the norms of society and what's construed as acceptable behavior. Sure it would be funny, but you can't bring yourself around to it. You're too professional, but it's not an easy decision especially when you know Bob's still drunk from the previous night's Tupperware party. That's one of the core issues with becoming a curmudgeon...we struggle with fitting into what's accepted and expected. Our instinct tells us one thing and our minds tell us another.

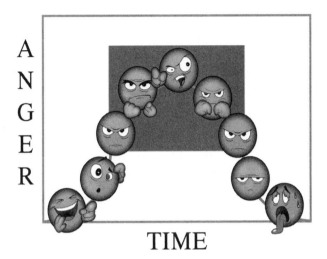

A
N
G
E
R

TIME

The Anger Box
Curmudgeons struggle with being professional and not
responding out of emotion. When you're in the red zone,
DON'T SAY ANYTHING!
Rational thought is next to impossible and you'll only regret
it.

Curmudgeon Quiz

You're in an elevator. Two people enter. One is wearing an Air Force flight suit. He says to his companion, "Defense Contractors are such slimeballs." Then they notice you and your bright yellow Defense Contractor badge and get quiet. They're caught talking shit and know it. You weigh the discretion option but determine this breach of tomfoolery deserves a response. You're only on the 1st floor and are going up to the 5th so there's time to strike back. Do you respond with:

a. "Bite me, Zoomie."

---

b. "And I hate Air Force Weenies who wear flight suits when they're not on flight status. I might as well wear Ron Jeremy's gold medallion and call myself The Hedgehog."
c. "And my momma always said if you're going to talk smack about someone make sure they're not standing right beside you."

While A is sooooo satisfying and B is true, C is the best answer because it's an emotionless and professional repost that leaves the target feeling stupid. Curmudgeon wins. Winston Churchill would be proud, for it was he who said: "Never hold discussions with the monkey when the organ grinder is in the room."

RESPECT
"I won't insult your intelligence by suggesting that you really believe what you just said."
-William F. Buckley Jr.

A curmudgeon's bitch trigger is quicker than an actor's relapse, so what's the determining factor between unleashing the wrath and bottling it up to release it on some other poor sap? Whether or not we respect the target. Remember Dave, the guy who wasn't wearing a tie when he should have been? Is Dave a good guy who works hard, doesn't complain, and distills his own bourbon? Did Dave strike out on his own to start a business and put everything into it only to have it fail because of something out of his control? Did he put his life on the line to stop a subway gang attack on a helpless old lady or carry a fallen comrade over miles of enemy desert to safety? Then there's a new variable in the equation: respect. The curmudgeon can stomach a slight apparel indiscretion committed by a respectable person. Is Dave a lazy kiss ass who falls asleep on the job and claims someone else's work as his own when he finally wakes up? The curmudgeon needs a volunteer for waterboarding training and Dave is it.

Respect is a two way street and to drive on it you have to earn your license. There are some people who don't and never will respect you. You can't win with them no matter how hard you try so just stop worrying about it and let them be. Curmudgeons are like honey badgers...we don't care what others think.

Example:
I knew a guy who was terrible at his job. Couldn't do anything right. Absolutely worthless. I didn't respect him at all, but then he took a new position in the company and suddenly he was a water walker. I heard people talk about what a great guy he was and thought, "Really? THAT guy? He sucked sweaty balls when I worked with him!" All I could see was the guy who couldn't do anything right so I never respected him and still don't to be honest. He may have excelled in a new environment but my perception will always of him being a bungling idiot.

That phenomenon works in reverse too. Plenty of people think I'm a total moron because they saw me at my worst while there are others who swear my tears will grow watermelons in the Sahara. All that matters is that the right people believe in you and the wrong ones fuck off.

Respect can't be forced and the savvy man will recognize when someone is trying to get him make himself be respected. Being subjected to every sad story whose objective is to make us respect someone is tiring. The media likes to build respect and/or an emotional connection by sensationalizing a backstory and to be honest it gets old.

Take any televised talent show like The X Factor or American Idol. The contestants with great voices are truly talented: but the ones with mediocre voices who have overcome some sort of diversity in their lives get so much more respect from the fans, because the editors spend a lot of time building up their connection to the audience through sympathy. A terminally ill kid in San Francisco wants to dress up like Batman and get a key to the city from the mayor and the entire city shows up, but if I put in a request for myself maybe my favorite delivery boy from Papa John's would be there, but that's it. Why? I'm healthy. I'm normal. I don't have anything in my life that would make you empathize or respect me. That's just the way it is in American entertainment.

Maybe this isn't a bad thing though. Maybe the internet has brought so many "you won't believe what this kid went through" stories that it's become common and we've stopped singling out people for being born with a disability or surviving a traumatic event. Maybe that's helping us accept everyone no matter what or who they are. Maybe this shows that people actually have compassion for those who have overcome an adversity more so than those who haven't.

But maybe it's also making us a culture where there's just no respect in being healthy or free of massive life-altering obstacles. I've worked my ass off to afford my family a stable, worry free life, but now I think my kids are fucked because of it. Children like mine who are raised in a healthy, happy, stable home don't have a great story of triumph to tell and will be put in the back of the respect line because of it. Should I get divorced so they have a reason to go to therapy or have something to cry about at parties? The media floods us with these feel good stories of resilient people who beat the odds so much that I want to drop my kids off in the woods a hundred miles from home and say "find your way back" so they have some sappy story to cry about. But I'd probably be arrested for child endangerment and I ain't going back to prison, Lieutenant Hanna.[7]

---

[7] Robert DeNiro, *Heat*

INDIVIDUALITY
"I'm free of all prejudices. I hate everyone equally."
-W.C. Fields

Those who believe every snowflake in the world is unique are fooling themselves. There are trillions upon kajillions of snowflakes falling on the earth at any given moment and each one goes through the same freezing process so to think that no two are alike is to ignore the basic laws of probability. It's water freezing into a crystalline pattern and there are only so many patterns in nature to choose from. The chances that there are two snowflakes whose structure is identical is the same as the possibility of life existing somewhere in the universe-very fucking high. There are trillions upon curmudgoenillions of galaxies and stars so the chance of life being out there somewhere is about 100%.

People are the same. There are 5 billion people in the world so the chances that there's someone very similar to you are high. That person may not be an exact twin, but you almost certainly fall into a category of some sort. As much as we like to think everyone is unique and beautiful, there are people whose actions make them easy to categorize because they think, feel, and do the same things that a group of others think, feel, and do. You're just not as special as you want to believe you are.

This is a good thing because it gives us a different perspective on individuality. By middle age we've learned there are equal parts decent people and worthless shits in every race, creed, color, church, state, town, village, and gym. We look at people in terms of respect and disrespect or admiration and apathy. We're very much a meritocracy demographic, meaning we like people who try and hate lazy shits no matter what their background. We believe that no one is owed anything and only hard work is worthy of a reward. We don't care about someone's physical makeup as much as their work ethic.

This is not an absolute. You can't say "well, I work hard, but I'm a pedophile when no one is looking, so I must be a good person." There are moral standards. For the most part, hard work is your ticket to curmudgeon respect, but only if you're not violating the basic laws of human goodness. Is it a gray area? Yes, but in the end everyone should be taken individually based on their own merits for a good reason: we've learned that stupidity and ignorance don't discriminate. They're everywhere.

PERSPECTIVE
"If you aren't in over your head, how do you know how tall you are?"
-T.S. Eliot

There's little in life more irritating than someone who doesn't have a proper perspective on life. Those fragile Pollyanna's of emotion that get shaken by the most innocuous of things (like someone who pisses their pants over a simple confrontation with a co-worker) are sickening. What they think is significant, isn't. There is a simple litmus test for perspective. When you think you're getting wrapped around the axle over something that does or doesn't matter, ask yourself six questions:

-Is anyone shooting at you?
-Do you have a terminal illness?
-Are you hopelessly addicted to anything?
-Are you homeless?
-Are you out of clean water?
-Are you starving?

If you can honestly answer no to all six questions then your life is better than 50% of the world. Suck it up and drive on. Quit your whining. It doesn't make any sense to worry over the little things when there are so many big, life-threatening ones that demand our attention and life energy.

Curmudgeonism stems from a fundamental belief that other people's opinions are flawed or just don't matter. You disapprove of me? Good for you. You're just another douchebag who's about as valuable as a condom machine in the Vatican. This isn't high school where the quarterback can laugh at a nerd and have all his sycophant sheep haze him into social damnation. This is real life and your opinions of us mean nothing, which has freed us up to say the things we want to. Curmudgeons accept this as a general truth of life and use it as a basis for what many believe is a generally bad temperament. But in reality it means we don't care about the people who don't matter, which is also the law of 25%.

The Law of 25% says one fourth of any audience will disagree with you no matter how genius or virtuous you are. Don't worry about them. Expect it and pay them no attention. Some people will reconsider their position if one single person disagrees with them. They haven't learned to stand their ground and haven't taken a moment in the shower to run a hand across his or her back and feel that thing called a spine. There will always be doubters but the true curmudgeon needs at least 25% dissonance before even thinking about changing his mind.

Example:

A man is watching a rugby game with 8 buddies and says, "that was a high tackle, he should be penalized" and 1-2 of them disagree (25% or less even by West Virginia math). At this point it's generally accepted that he is correct and he needs not worry about the dissenting opinions. However, if 3-4 disagree (up to 50%) then he should keep an open mind on the situation. If 5-6 disagree then he should seriously reconsider his position and if 7-8 disagree he's drunk.

A related theory is that 25% of the people we meet in life think we're worthless and weak and nothing we do will change that perception. Some people make flash judgments that last forever. If you don't impress them in the first minute of meeting then you're screwed forever. They will write you off as less valuable than a screen door on a submarine and nothing you do will ever engender a full recovery. Along those same lines, there are some people who are easily impressed and will think you're absolutely awesome no matter what even after 15 seconds of knowing them. Forget both types. Nothing you say or do will change their position and therefore they don't matter. They are set in their opinions so it makes no sense to waste your time to try to change them. Keep a realistic perspective and move on. There are billions of people in this world so getting upset about one person's opinion about you is insane.

Part of keeping a sound perspective on life is not being enamored with people who think they're changing the world but aren't. I'm talking about entertainers. Entertainers are just that...entertainers. Actors, musicians, and (to a lesser extent) athletes and authors are here for one purpose only: to entertain us.

There's nothing wrong with dedicating your life to the arts and perfecting your craft and in some cases celebrities use their status for good and we applaud them for that. But they're not to be worshipped or blindly followed as leaders or world changers. They're not policymakers, scientists, doctors, pioneers, astronauts, generals, law enforcement, or have any real impact on anything other than providing us with a momentary escape from life. Without our dollars, they'd be on a subway street corner playing for handouts to spend on coffee to get the energy jolt they need to get up and do it again. Their commitment to their profession is laudable, but if a zombie apocalypse suddenly happened today they'd be bait.

A famous actress once said, "It's only through movies that we learn who we are." Nothing could be more hornswaggle bullshit. It's through love, loss, pain, joy, birth, death, war, peace, adversity, embarrassment, failure, success, pushing your boundaries, honing your abilities, getting knocked down and getting back up again and telling the world, 'you hit like a bitch' that we learn who we are. An occasional motion picture will capture some of that experience, but it's only a tiny fraction of the process of self-discovery. That's life's job, not Hollywood's.

While we're talking about entertainers, it's a hard sell to feel an emotional outpouring for one (or anyone successful for that matter) when they succumb to drug addiction or other vice. These are people who actively seek a life that's void of personal privacy and under constant scrutiny with easy access to a buffet of dangerous addictions run by ambitious and unscrupulous businessmen who give two fucks about their personal well being. When you're paid millions of dollars to act on a stage or play a game and throw it all away for something so obscure that you should have seen coming, you're just weak. Get some perspective and realize how good you have it.

This is not to say curmudgeons think they are the most important people in the world. We're definitely not convinced of our own superiority and in fact we recognize there are people who can do many things better than us and WANT them to do so and therefore push people to be better. We want this world (that we have limited time left in) to be a better place to live, so we give our opinions when the people who aren't doing it fail. We hate laziness and respect ambition and drive. We have a solid perspective on who we are and just want others to do the same.

EXPECTATIONS
"Lay low, play dumb, keep moving"
-Roger Stone

Closely tied to perspective is expectation. Listen up...come closer to the page...if there's one area that all young people should be educated on, it's this. Expectations cut several ways. People expect things of you and you expect things of them and when those expectations aren't met we get disappointed, mad, violent, depressed, and build headless snowmen that horrify the neighborhood.

This is important. Put down your cocktail and pay attention. DON'T EVER over-inflate someone's expectations. Manage them. If you tell your neighbor you can get Van Halen to play his kid's graduation party and don't come through, you'll go from savior to goat in a nanosecond. "Under-promise and over-deliver" is a rule everyone should live by. Don't promise jack shit unless you can deliver it and conversely don't believe everyone else's snake oil cure-alls and promises of Ponzi returns. Be skeptical of people so when they fail (and they will) it's no big deal.

Example:
American McKayla Maroney was picked to win a gold medal HANDS DOWN in the event that she owned for several years leading up to the 2012 Olympics, the vault. So her expectations (and everyone's really) were astronomically high going into the games right up until the moment that shit happened. She slipped and fell on the final attempt and got a silver medal. She accepted her silver like a curmudgeon; with a scowl and contempt. But wait...anyone would kill for an Olympic silver medal right? Not her. Why? Because her expectations were higher. For the rest of her life she will look at something anyone else would be incredibly proud of with nothing but disgust, a reminder of her failure because her expectations were off. How sad.

Curmudgeons have low expectations in others and deservedly so. We've been duped, misled, and over-excited about a widget that sounded like the next great thing but turned into vapor. We've experienced loss and in turn have lost faith in people who over-promised so therefore we know that getting our hopes up is a bad idea that will likely end in disappointment. We keep our expectations of others low because we know the world will just let us down in the end more often than it will impress us.

So what about when we look inside? What do you do when your life doesn't meet your own expectations or doesn't even come close to them? Does anyone's life meet their expectations? Probably, but it's more an exception than a rule. So do the 95% of us who don't do as well in life as we hoped to just wallow in self-pity in a dark room or do we keep trying to make our lives better?

On the one hand it's human nature to be envious of what someone else has, but on the other hand, begrudging someone their success is petty. It can be devastating to look around and see other people achieving what you wanted to, especially when you have a friend who's living your dream life. But so what if someone else did all the things you wanted to? That's no reason to hate him for it.

Reason says we're supposed to do the manly, right thing - suck it up, smile, say 'I'm happy for you' and move on. But we're humans and we're prone to those pesky emotions. We want to be the best or have the most, therefore the benevolent man is the one who overcomes his spite and says congratulations. Americans love to win but hate a winner. Someone else is leading a charmed life and we get jealous and want that charmed life ourselves. In reality we need to suck it up and build our own. In the end, if your life sucks then you have no one else to blame but yourself for making bad decisions or having unachievable expectations.

STANDARDS

"Private Joker is silly and he's ignorant, but he's got guts and guts is enough."

-Gunnery Sergeant Hartman

"Enlisted men drink beer. Officers drink bourbon," my curmudgeon father told me many times growing up, clearly disappointed in my affection for cereal malt beverage. His message wasn't so much about being better than the enlisted man and, in fact, he was always the first one to promote the benevolent Foot Soldier as the most virtuous man on earth. But he had an old-world chivalric way about him and knew where the line was between the ranks. In my day just about every officer drank beer, but that wasn't the point. Pop's message was much larger than the beverage of choice. It was all about standards.

People aspire to gradually increase their quality of life little by little, year by year and raise their standards. There's nothing wrong with that. In our twenties, driving an old beater car and eating Spaghetti-O's out of the can in a dorm room was just fine. By middle age it's a cold day in hell when either of those things happen. It's sad to say, but cutting corners, not trying as hard as I could, and accepting sub-standard work was fine once in a while back then. Now we demand more of ourselves and everyone else. There's a standard to keep and we don't want to back off of it (notice I didn't say 'won't ever back off' because compromise happens - see the next section).

There's a difference between standards and expectations. Expectations are things you want to achieve in the future, but standards are set by things in the past. Standards are usually based on actual events while expectations are based on hope. A silver spoon teenager raised on Fifth Avenue has a standard of dining in 5-star restaurants and an expectation that he will always be able to do so. Whether or not that happens is up to him.

Just like expectations, some people set their standards too high. While the Occupy Wall Street movement was raging against the machine and claiming there were no jobs for college grads, millions of openings stayed unfilled. The youthful protestors didn't want to accept an entry-level job because they thought they were better than that, and maybe some of them were. But if you want a job and there's an open job then take the damn job and quit whining. This isn't rocket surgery. Setting ridiculously high standards is a recipe for failure unless living in your mom's basement and eating tuna fish is an acceptable life.

Curmudgeon Quiz
You're sparring with a friend (let's assume you've thrown a punch at some time in your life even if you haven't). He's slacking. His punches are weak and he keeps dropping his hands. Do you:

a). Say "you're clearly not into this today so let's go get a latte and a bran muffin.
b). Let him hit you in the face to build his sagging confidence.
c). Punch him square in the nose and follow it up with a legkick that's borderline on the testes.

The answer is C. If I hit you during sparring then that's my way of saying I give a shit because it's my job as your sparring partner to prepare you for a real fight. If your defense is whimsical and your strikes are weaker than Dakota Fanning's then it's my responsibility to get you to tighten your shit up and pain is a great teacher. Tough standards save lives. Iron forges iron so if you can't hang then get out of the ring and sell shoes. If you don't quit then I'll be ecstatic, but I'll test you until you do.

PRAGMATISM
"If God did not intend for us to eat animals then why did he make them out of meat?"
-John Cleese

Revolution is great fun until there's a body count. Or as the great orator William F. Buckley said, "Idealism is fine, but as it approaches reality, the costs become prohibitive." By middle age we have seen the way the world works and have experienced loss, setback, failure, and even catastrophic defeat, so excuse us if we don't believe in your great idea to make flying cars. It's not that we don't trust in your drive and ambition but we've stuck our fingers in the bike spokes and lost them once or twice already. The line between fantasy and reality is not a fine one, but rather a great chasm, and you can only live on one side or the other.

Those who expect the world to be perfectly harmonious and peaceful are living in denial and don't understand that there will always be people who are aggressive and want to wage war. It's human nature to want what someone else has and resort to violence to get it. It will never go away until we live in the brave new world of gene engineering. To think it will change naturally is blind ignorance.

Curmudgeons get frustrated with people who deny reality. There's the world we want to live in and the one we actually DO live in. Illegal immigrants live in America in large numbers. Accept it instead of wishing them away. If you want them to go away then make them citizens, create an Alien Tax and set it at 50%. They'll leave lickety split. Drugs are here to stay whether you like it or not. Legalize it, isolate it, control it, and tax it. Drug violence will disappear, addiction will decline, and the government will be wealthy again.

As much as we like to think democracy is the greatest form of government ever, there are peoples who need the iron fist of tyranny to keep them in line. Tito kept Yugoslavia (a tapestry of disparate tribes if ever there was one) civil and as soon as he was gone it free fell into the abyss of bloodthirsty civil war and horrifying genocide. As big of a prick as Saddam Hussein was, he kept Shias and Sunnis from slaughtering each other for a long time through terror tactics that worked. Some people are morally bankrupt and unable to comprehend freedom as anything other than a license to kill the people they hate. Give them an inch and they'll make a mile of blood. Quite wishing it didn't happen. It does.

So let's flip the coin and practice what we preach. Let's try to understand the people we just can't. Maybe it's unrealistic to think that curmudgeons can prod or motivate people into action. There will always be those who are lazy and refuse to get off of welfare and work no matter how much we give them the tools to do so. In their case the government has to take care of them because they're unable to take care of themselves and therefore welfare is a benevolent program. In that sense maybe it's also unrealistic to think that illegal aliens should pay taxes and if we banned drugs no one would be able to abuse them. How's that been working out so far?

ACCOUNTABILITY
"Ninety-nine percent of all failures come from people who have a habit of making excuses."
-George Washington Carver

It's naïve balderdash to think everyone has some sense of responsibility and accountability for their actions. For each stand-up person you're proud to know there's an unscrupulous jackhole whose worthlessness contaminates the herd like a cancer. These irresponsible shits who try to make someone else look bad instead of taking responsibility for their actions themselves are a major source of the curmudgeon's angst. People who avoid blame instead of taking it are part of the reason we are who we are; because we've been hit by the bullets they've dodged. There's a very specific order to the way we want the world to be and the people who don't have any moral accountability keep fucking it up.

It's a benign example but "I'm just sayin'" illustrates this point. It's got to be the stupidest phrase ever. People use "I'm just sayin'" to avoid the repercussions of opening their mouths, like they think any offensive remark can be forgiven by adding "I'm just sayin'" on the end of it. It's a hollow get out of jail free card that the naïve honor.
Example:

"Dude, your mom's hot I want to poke her."

"What? That's offensive. I'm going to kick your ass."

"I'm just sayin'."

"Oh, okay. As long as you're just sayin' then it's all good."

How is this acceptable in a society where people are supposed to take responsibility for their actions? The answer: it's not and that's the point. People today (especially teens) don't want to stand up and defend the things they say. They won't stand their ground and shout, "That's right! I said it. Whatcha gonna do about it bitch?"[8]

Being accountable for your actions and/or admitting when you've said something you truly believe in even when it ruffles feathers is admirable. Got caught with your hand in the cookie jar? Own it. Got elected on promises you couldn't keep? No one to blame but yourself. Wrote an opinionated book that polarized a demographic?

[8] Everything is funnier with "bitch" on the end of it.

Defend it. If you fucked up, say you fucked up instead of trying to pin your failure on someone else. Don't pass the buck if it stops with you.

I'm just sayin.'

HAPPINESS

"Happy," I muttered, trying to pin the word down. But it is one of those words, like Love, that I have never quite understood.

-Hunter S. Thompson

Think you're owed happiness? You're not. Happiness is a luxury, not a necessity. Some say "if you're not happy doing what you're doing then don't do it." Those people are surprisingly more comfortable with a welfare Christmas and a moped than the average person. It's idealistic, but many times unrealistic and as we've learned already, idealism has a cost.

The definition of happiness is different for everyone but one thing is for sure-it's fleeting. Just when you think you're on the verge of a touchdown, the goal line moves. The variables change and suddenly you're on a quest to make it to the next level of happiness. Even then, you can accomplish your mission in life and buy a nice house, nice cars, and a baby giraffe and feel happy but then you realize you have to protect it. You have everything you wanted and a life that's enviable. That means you have to maintain it. You have to keep it going. That adds pressure and makes you unhappy again. It's a vicious cycle.

The universe does not owe anyone a single atom of happiness and there's no law that says you have to love your chosen profession. As long as a job provides income and necessities for the family then it can suck badger milk because true happiness for a man comes from being a provider. It's our responsibility to take care of our kin and we want to fulfill that responsibility no matter how happy or unhappy it makes us. Curmudgeons sacrifice the happiness of the self for the needs of the family because we're not egotistical or narcissistic.

Some Deepak Chopra Zen master schmuck will tell you that you have to be happy in life or that you should continually strive to find greater levels of happiness. That works for some, but if you're a family man then you have the responsibility to provide for those you love and that's it. If you're not happy but you're providing a good life then suck it up, cupcake.

My soul dies a little each day at work, but I provide a comfortable living for my family therefore I will be its punching bag and shut up and take it. Some days I hate what I've become but then I step through the doors of my house and it's all washed away. Coming home from a day on the job is like finishing a hard ass gym workout. It sucked, but in the end it's satisfying to know my sacrifice had a purpose and my good health means I will live to work another day and my family will be good to go a little longer. Men are wired to provide, even if it's just for ourselves, and when anything threatens our ability to do that we freak out just a little bit.

On the grand scale of things happiness is a want, not a need. We *need* to provide. We *want* to be happy but if we're not happy, but we're providing then that's a form of happiness in itself or at the very least a form of satisfaction. I may not fit some liberal's view of happy but I'm content and that's good enough for me. Don't agree? Quit your crappy job just to spite me. It's not easy is it? Show me a job that pays as much as I'm making now that I can enjoy and then I'll listen to your "don't work in a job you hate" argument. Otherwise leave me alone. I have a family to provide for.

TRUST

"In a world full of thieves the final sin is stupidity."
-Hunter S. Thompson

"Men have trust issues!" Not gonna argue with that, so let's think about why. We're in our mid-forties and have had a lot of time to interact with a lot of people who only care abut themselves and will take advantage of you faster than Lindsey Lohan rapes a mini bar. Curmudgeons trust their inner circle of family and friends, but are very reluctant to put trust in anyone who hasn't proven themselves. We trust, but it's selective and we're always prepared to be disappointed. Cause it happens a lot.

When crossing the street with children I never trust that a car will stop no matter how cherry red the light is and how blaze orange my pants are. An oncoming driver can even stop and wave me on, but I'll still watch them like a hawk and I'm always ready to grab my kids and sprint to the curb in case his brake foot slips. In this case it's "trust but verify."

Because we're skeptics at heart, we REALLY don't trust the person who provides a quick answer to a question because it's frequently the wrong one. I'll take a slow, methodical, correct piece of information over a quick, wrong one any day. We've all seen that guy. He's usually young and ambitious and eager to please so he can charm his way up the corporate ladder. He'll sacrifice accuracy for speed and will never earn a solid trustworthy reputation for being correct because he's too focused on being first. He's a snake. Give him a wide berth so his mediocrity doesn't rub off on you.

The least trustworthy people of all are those who don't dream of glory. Everyone should strive to improve their lot in life even if it's just by a tiny increment. That doesn't mean everyone should be overly ambitious, but there's not point in sitting stagnant and waiting for death.

When you close your eyes do you dream of failure? Not unless you're the type who's only happy when he's miserable in which case please pitch a tent where no one can hear you cry yourself to sleep. Most people dream of doing something you can't do in real life. Whether that's winning a World Series in the bottom of the ninth or meeting the love of your life, it's still an endstate that leaves you better off than you are now. That's glorious. Don't trust anyone who says they don't wish for something better.

COMMITMENT
"Success consists of going from failure to failure without loss of enthusiasm."
-Winston Churchill

The show must go on. It doesn't matter how sick you are, how sore you are, how uncomfortable you are after a bad breakup with a co-worker, get your striped ass to your place of business and show the world that the little things can't beat you. Those who overcome obstacles to stay on the right path are to be respected and the ones who get distracted by something shiny are to be mocked.

Committing to anything is easy when you're cozy, but takes serious intestinal fortitude when things get uncomfortable. That goes for almost anything in life. Committing to a diet sounds like a great idea when your stomach is full. It's when you're hungry that it gets hard. Save money when your account is full? Easy. Save when you're broke? Hard. Be faithful to your spouse when times are good? Easy. Keep your eyes in your head and hands to yourself when she's being a hardcore bitch? Hard.

Staying committed to something when it seems like there's no reason to be is how we learn our limits. It's also how we learn judgment because let's be honest, there are some things that it doesn't pay to stay committed to. Did you faithfully follow the Seahawks believing that one day they'd eventually win a Superbowl? Good for you for showing the patience to wait 30 years for that. Staying on the Titanic until rescue arrives? Bad idea. Committed to holding onto Apple stock when Steve Jobs died? Good idea. Hanging on to Enron stock at anytime, ever? You get an A for commitment and an F for judgment.

Overall we respect those who are committed more than the Fairweather Johnsons who bend like a reed in the river, but don't let commitment blind you into driving headlong into a disaster. Have the situational awareness to recognize when you're standing at the crossroads of good commitment and bad judgment.

Commitment for curmudgeons means having something to fight for. It's one reason we're so surly; we have something we want to protect and are easily irritated when someone or something threatens that. We feel it's important to commit ourselves to something. It can be a wife, a family, a friend, an idea, the military, religion, politics, your nest egg, Area 51, Sasquatch hunting, a precious ring, whatever. There's nothing wrong with committing your loyalty to something and dedicating yourself to protecting or growing it. There are people (including curmudgeons) who drift across the ocean of life on threadbare rafts, unable to commit to dry land for no reason. That's pathetic, but it's their life, not mine.

FAILURE
"If at first you don't succeed, try, try again.
Then quit. There's no point in being a damn fool about it."
-WC Fields

Failure is a defining human characteristic that sears a black brand on most men's souls. Defeat leaves us with feelings of inadequacy and doubt and many times fuels biblical revenge for the violent at heart or redemption for those who seek to wash an ugly stain from the fabric of their lives. Though there are certainly those who enjoy showering in their own pity each morning, the great many of us think failure is like a nerve gas; a tortuous thing to be avoided at all costs.

Enough of that. If you have to be told that failing sucks then you've either never failed at anything (unlikely), have no soul (is your nickname Mephistopheles?), never taken a chance (leave the house once in while, dude), or are deliriously fooling yourself (you're Tenth Place trophy is actually the world's way of saying you failed).

I've heard many men say "the further I get into my forties the more I think about my failures." Been there. Is this nature's spiteful way of making us regret our lives before we die? Human life expectancy used to be much shorter before the miracle of modern medicine and distilled sprits. We used to only live to age 40, 45, or 50 if you led a stress free life of doing nothing. It's only been in the last century that life expectancies have moved into the seventies, which is just a blip on the universe's radar. Instinct hasn't had a chance to catch up, so feelings of regret and reminders of failure could be nature's way of telling us that we're about to die and it's time to repent our sins. It's like male menopause only we apologize for everything instead of ripping people's faces off.

Regret is usually born of bad decisions and is the only emotion that can elicit immediate sadness and fond reminiscence at the same time. It brings back the past powerfully, mostly because the events associated with regret are failures caused by either hesitation or recklessness that etch themselves too clearly into the mind. We all regret something and would change the past were it possible. The person who says "I don't regret a thing" is full of shit. Old folks say it, but mostly because they can no longer remember when their dad caught them poking a hole in the mattress and used the old, "I was going to hide something in it" excuse. Yeah...your weenie!

Back to failure...there are two clear schools of thought when you're staring defeat in the face:

1. Never give up.
2. The universe is trying to tell you something.

Option 1 is almost always correct. Whether you're a POW in the Hanoi Hilton or a contestant on the Amazing Race, never give up. Unrelenting persistence is one of the things that gets us to old age.

As for option 2, there's definitely a time to throw in the towel. Some idealist will tell you, "Just believe and keep trying and you'll get there" while a realist will say, "It's never gonna happen. Stop now." In every situation one is correct, but it's rarely clear until it's clear. Does this sound familiar? Remember the passage about commitment just one page ago?

Really it's all situation-dependent and only a healthy dose of reality will illuminate the correct path. Do you realistically have a chance of making the USA basketball team at age 47? No, and no matter how much you believe in yourself it will never happen because you physically can't keep up. Stop now. Could you be a bestselling author someday? Yes. Believe in yourself, work hard, and keep trying.

Failure is rarely more pronounced in someone's life than in sports. Missed that buzzer beater jumpshot that could have won the game? You'll never live it down even long after everyone else has forgotten it. But ironically it's easier to respect someone who's lost more than someone who's never courted the bitter bitch of defeat. A 10-1 record is more than impressive than 10-0. The fighter who's grinded out a slobberknocker and felt the unrelenting pain of loss will grow and evolve more than the fighter who's blissfully unaware of the suffering that comes with watching someone else's hand being raised in victory.

SPORTS

"Serious sport has nothing to do with fair play. It is bound up with hatred, jealousy, boastfulness, disregard of all rules and sadistic pleasure in witnessing violence. In other words, it is war minus the shooting."
-George Orwell

If there's one thing in this book that will put people into the stratosphere it's this section because Americans love sports and have polarizing views on professional athletes. So put your tray tables up and prepare for lift off.

America would be a much more influential competitor on the international sports scene without the NFL and MLB. Our best athletes are trained from birth to aspire to be at the elite level of American football and baseball because that's where the money is and what's more American than making money, right? Unfortunately no one plays American football outside North America and only a few countries play baseball. Every time the NFL has tried to export itself or expand it has failed and baseball only enjoyed a limited run in the Olympics because no one really cared about it in the end. These games are inherently American and will never be global sports for so many more reasons than you care to hear me babble about.

And yet our best athletes flock to these sports and leave the other ones in which the rest of the world competes void of truly great talent. Without the NFL the USA would have linebackers pushing bobsleds down Europe's throat, wide receivers destroying decathlons, and running backs running through soccer.

It's embarrassing watching the USA Rugby team lose to Tonga, Fiji, and Kenya when we have such incredible athletes who dedicate their lives to other sports at an early age and can't spell rugby. But it will never change because at its core, American football and baseball are just that...American. They're specific to a limited number of countries and as such we take pride in our top two sports being unique and isn't that what made America in the first place? Breaking away from the rest of the world and being who we want to be? Piss off all you Euro-wankers!

As long as the best American athletes are drawn to these two sports, we will be a second rate international power in almost everything else...which, I'm not saying is a bad thing, but is something we have to get used to. For the rest of the world this is a good thing. They're happy that we're distracted with our national sports and shudder at the thought of Julius Peppers, Derek Jeter, or Clay Matthews playing one of the games they succeed in. The mighty New Zealand All Blacks rugby team, one of the most dominate forces in all sports, would be threatened by the wakened giant that is America. We would create a crushing scrum, an impenetrable defense, and a tornado of violence that ripped through anyone and everyone we faced. Every sport would become like Olympic basketball where our Dream Team cruises to victory with blindfolds (usually). What a world that would be, but this is one of those things that will never happen so we just have to accept it and move on.

I think the US Customs and Border Patrol Agency is ruled by soccer fans who want to see us win a World Cup someday so they secretly let every Mexican in and hope for amnesty. Because if we naturalized every illegal alien in America we would have the same success in soccer as we do in war.

69

I used to get pissed when the USA got bounced out of international competitions like the FIFA World Cup. After all it's not easy to stomach watching your national team get schooled by Ghana or Costa Rica. But then I thought about it and came to conclusion that we shouldn't give a shit about it because soccer is a poor man's sport. It takes nothing more than a goat's head and two sticks so anyone in the poorest Brazilian favela or Indian slum can play it and America doesn't have as many poor as the rest of the world.

The uniquely North American sports - American Football, Baseball, Hockey, Lacrosse - these all take pads, sticks, helmets, and equipment that costs money. Money we can afford but most of the rest of the world can't, so they don't play our sports. Or they just don't get us.

I don't hate soccer, but I dislike soccer players because they dive. The dive is a way of acting like you're hurt so the ref will call a penalty on the other team and give you an advantage. In this way the diver is A) cheating and B) attempting to get someone else to win the game because he can't do it himself. This is like being a prison bitch so you get protection from the truly powerful Bubba's of the yard.

Soccer is a culture of fakers and cheaters but even more insidious is how they take all the credit for success and none of the blame for failure. When a soccer player scores a goal he runs and celebrates and holds his arms out to the crowd like he's Jesus and the fans are his righteous flock but when a mistake is made they point fingers at each other and yell "Not my fault! Yours!" Worthless.

Professional athletes and ego go hand in hand and when the outspoken ones lose, we love it because Americans love to win but hate a winner. Who doesn't revel in watching the humble man with a good backstory take a victory lap around the asshole who wrongly predicted a win and deserves a dose of cheesy smothered crow. It's the universe's way of balancing the idiots of the outer ring with the decent folk of the middle layer.

There are few things as offensive to us as the big time athlete who thinks he's better than everyone else. American sports are a machismo world of 'look at me' with an endless supply of financially fueled self-importance. That's not to say all athletes fall into this cesspool of attitude, but the ones who do ruin a lot of the glamour of sports for the ones who don't. And yet, we can't stop watching. It's enthralling and exciting and sometimes we watch just to get a glimpse of train wrecks that make us feel better about ourselves. Thank God for live TV.

Think about this. Football players celebrate after making a tackle, sacking the QB or just catching a ball for a small gain, but isn't that their job? They jump up and proclaim their might to the world like they killed a terrorist on his way to an elementary school, but isn't that what they're paid five times the average American salary to do? Weren't they hired to tackle, sack, catch, and score?

What if we all did that? What if we all celebrated after doing the things we're paid to do? I'd be like, "I sent that email like a mother fucker! That's right internet bitch! I gave my opinion to that guy like a gangsta! Go home suit! You can't fuck with me!" My wife would come home from dropping the kids off at school and get flagged for excessive celebration every damn day.

On the opposite end of the spectrum, why does an athlete being Christian suddenly make him a good person? We see an athlete genuflect or give thanks to God and suddenly there's an assumption that he's got a heart of gold and saves puppies from a garbage crusher in his off time. If he praises Jesus then he must be a good person and we want to see him win so his twitter account doubles. Meanwhile, the FBI's own profile of a typical serial killer says "he is usually very religious just before starting his killing spree." Cue the creepy psycho music.

SECURITY
"The strength of the pack is the wolf. And the strength of the wolf is the pack."
-Rudyard Kipling

There's a feeling of superiority that comes with sitting in a warm, dry house eating steak and drinking purified water on a cold, rainy day when all the animals of the world are foraging for scraps and dying of dysentery. It reassures us of our place at the top of the food chain and underscores the need for reason and adaptation. Sure humans get eaten by predators every year, but only the dumb ones who think they can swim with sharks, live with bears, or put their heads in the mouth of a crocodile. They're idiots who mistakenly convince themselves they can form some kind of surreal bond with an unthinking animal. Their deaths just make the human race stronger. Natural selection is alive and well.

Eating animals reminds us of our primal side when we had to chase down our meals and gnaw through a tough exterior hide to get to the raw meat of a fresh kill. It reminds us how far we've come as a species. We so completely dominate the food chain that we can casually raise livestock, fowl, and fish for the day we feel compelled to eat it with yummy sauces, fresh guacamole, and a mariachi band. This security is really what people need to be prosperous in a civilized society. Elections are cool, but they don't provide a community with what it really needs: the security of knowing that you can walk to the corner Stop 'N Rob and buy a six pack without getting shot at. It's what people need to be productive and ultimately happy.

Security can be as inane as the soothing sounds of lawn care equipment on a weekend that says "Suburbia is fine. All is well." The thought that so many people prioritize something so trivial as the height of their grass and the shape of their shrubberies fills us with the feeling of security and reinforces the blanket of successful capitalism that we cuddle up into every night. There's something gratifying about raging a battle against weeds instead of against another tribe for food. Security is truly the cornerstone of everything else we do.

TECHNOLOGY
"I won't be impressed with technology until I can download food."
-Anonymous

It's only a matter of time before drones become like smart phones. Everyone will have one because the need to know what's going on at all hours of the day and night no matter what the distance is an all-consuming obsession with people. Just look at the internet and cell phones. What is the real purpose of these things? To acquire information as fast as possible.

A drone does that. It can hover over anything and transmit visual and audio data back to the operator in real time. Want to stalk your ex? Buy a drone. Want to rob a house? Buy a drone. Want to make an anonymous cash drop to a hit man? Buy a drone. And what will all this drone activity lead to? The erosion of security. You won't know when you're being watched and when you're not but you will always assume someone has a mosquito-sized drone buzzing around your house, so you will take measures to guard against it, like blackened out windows and transmission jammers so the signal can't make it back to the operator.

So now is the time to invest in a drone-busting company that will someday invent a radar-based device that detects and shoots down any drone that breaches your property. Of course version 1 will also shoot down every bird in the neighborhood, but that's the price of security. And security is really what we need for a prosperous society. Deep down we all need the security of knowing that we can drive across a bridge without it collapsing or walk down to the local Stop 'N Rob convenience store to buy a Mountain Dew without being shot at or spied on and will pay any price to ensure that security.

Technology will balance out the gene pool because it's only a matter of time before our need to know everything in real time will combine with the creative geniuses of capitalism and we're all wearing our computers on our face. Microtechnologies will make it possible to put an entire laptop into the same space as a pair of sunglasses so we can text, email, watch the news, and of course surf porn while driving. That will lead to more automobile accidents caused by ADD horn dogs jerking off in the driver's seat. Manslaughter by boner will become a new crime. Darwinism will claim more idiots and the universe will be in balance again. Thank you, Microsoft.

POLITICS & GOVERNMENT
"The art of public life consists to a great extent of knowing where to stop and going a bit further."
-Saki

When a man goes into politics his soul belongs to someone else and his heart is merely an impersonal possession. He doesn't really represent the people he pretends to. He represents a small, influential fraction of his constituency that got him elected to which he's indebted. To think otherwise is folly. Curmudgeons don't expect much from politicians (as we don't from the general population) and we're never disappointed. They keep aiming at nothing and hitting it.

It would be nice to think curmudgeons are apolitical; that Republicans, Democrats, Libertarians and Tea Party-ers can be equally as curmudgeonly as the next guy. But deep down that's stretching the truth. Curmudgeons are crotchety bastards who lean inherently to the right. We believe in individual responsibility, small government, small business, the right to bear arms, national pride, no handouts, and most importantly the right to determine our own destiny. Those are usually conservative views.

The good news is politics and religion are like food. What's delicious and satisfying to one is stinky tofu puke to another. Even though we don't agree with many ideologies (and even hold some in quiet contempt), we are very much a live and let live demographic so if you believe in bestiality and isolationism, that's fine. We'll quietly hate you, but let you live in your world while we live in ours as long as you stay off our lawn.

The number one most important function of the US government is to set the conditions for the citizenry to succeed, not tell us what to do or how to live our lives. Period. We want government to let us decide how to spend our days and let us fend for ourselves. Just create the conditions for security, fairness, and prosperity and get out of the way. Our personal space is our personal space and we don't want you in it. That doesn't mean we believe in vigilante law and want to live on a mountain and shoot at anyone who comes close, but we believe in being part of a functioning, prosperous society without being overregulated. Some would say then that curmudgeons are civil libertarians and therefore Democrats, which could have a nugget of truth to it (albeit a small one), but I'll leave this one up to you. Curmudgeonism is not parochial.

Government and business are diametrically opposed. One is designed to make money and the other is designed to spend it. One is efficient. The other hopelessly lost in waste. In the business world you have to maximize profit and find ways to save and make money. In government you have to spend your budget or you don't get it the following year, so at the end of every fiscal year there's a mad scramble to exodus federal funds to get the cash off the books no matter how silly the expenditure. It's a sordid dance between the people who create wealth and the organization that absorbs it. This also creates a dangerous environment of low standards. "Good enough for government work" is supposed to be a joke, but when you work around government the sad, sobering reality is this is truth. There are several reasons for this phenomenon:

-It doesn't have to be efficient or even good. The government is in no danger of going away so it doesn't need people who are going to ensure its longevity.
-The government is not profit oriented so it doesn't need creative, innovative people to find ways to make money. It's not like a business that has to make money or everyone loses their job or a colony where everyone works their asses off to prevent cannibalism and death by hatchet. Without a life-or-death motive there's no incentive to find ways to survive, which stifles creativity. Any action taken is good enough. The impetus to produce or be fired is removed from the equation so they can be mediocre forever with no repercussions.
-Hiring standards are lower because you don't have to prove that you've accomplished anything. You don't have to

show how effective you've been in the past like taking a start up business from zero to kajillions or launched an innovative campaign to make unicorns popular. You just have to show that you know how to breathe. And government background checks? Those are pencil drills that are easily manipulated.
-It's nearly impossible to fire someone from government service. True story - a man in a government agency was streaming porn for 6 hours a day on a government computer but when his supervisor tried to fire him it took 6 months, a two-inch thick file of violations and hundreds of hours of legal counsel. Even then he still got a new job with a different government agency. When you know it's nearly impossible to get fired and have no motivation to make serious change in an organization, then it becomes too easy to resort to basic human laziness. Government workers are wholly comfortable and have no reason to actually work.
-The government's main job is to spend money or ensure that others are spending government funds. Any monkey can do that and yet wasteful spending practices surface all the time. The government's business model is spend spend spend instead of make make make or be fired for not making. That creates an environment of failure.

Now I'm not going to say every government employee fits into this description and yes, our government does produce beneficial outcomes once in a while. But on the whole its standards for personnel are low and it doesn't operate in an environment of kill or be killed (or even survival of the fittest) so it's a lethargic organization of inefficiency and wastefulness. There's no motivation to use your skills or to really do anything at all other than the bare minimum. Even then the chances of being terminated are slim, so the next time you hear someone say "it's a government conspiracy" think about how inept our government truly is and you'll realize it's not capable of one. It just does what's good enough for government work and nothing more.

Anyone who believes in government conspiracies has never worked in government and has no idea how frightfully ill-equipped the government is to execute one in any sort of efficient or secret manner. They couldn't develop a conspiracy much less keep one quiet if their pensions depended on it. If you've ever worked one day in or around the government you wouldn't believe a single conspiracy theory. They're just not smart enough to pull one off.

If anything stirs the curmudgeon to action it's the government budget. We take interest in the budget more than any other government function. Why? Because we're the ones paying taxes and want to know how they're being spent. Only honest Joes file tax returns. Those who make their money illegally don't pay taxes and get the benefit of public services at the expense of the law-abiding citizens. You're a drug dealer who made millions off of street crack? Paying taxes would be tantamount to admitting guilt, so don't do it but by all means send your kids to the school that the honest people paid for. Like the smooth roads in your neighborhood, well equipped hospital a few miles away, and the trained military that defends you? You're welcome.

The notion that honest Americans are punished for being law-abiding citizens through IRS scrutiny is revolting, but curmudgeons accept it and use that angst to funnel our attention toward government accountability. If criminals are going to live a tax-free life with all the benefits we have, then we have the right to insist that our tax dollars are spent bringing them to justice. In a curmudgeon's world this is supply and demand. We supply the government with money and then demand they use it properly.

Personally I'd rather be taxed when I spend money instead of when I make it. That way I decide when and how the government gets paid. As it is they take my money whether I like it or not and the harder I work the bigger cut they take. The current system of tax and spend (even if you don't want them to) ends up absorbing wealth instead of creating it.

If the government even hints at taking firearms people go ape shit, but when they openly declare that they're going to take your money no one cares. When was the last time government took your guns? Never. When was the last time they took your money? Today.

And every day you buy something.

And every time you get a paycheck.

And when you get married

And even when you die.

They're called taxes and they're everywhere.

The government constantly absorbs the wealth we accumulate and no one complains no matter how absurd the tax is, but even whisper "gun confiscation" and the torrent of almighty hellfire is unleashed. Don't get me wrong, I own guns and like them. But the incredible fervor with which people defend the 2nd Amendment should be channeled into defending their pocketbooks.

Why? Because it's the free market economy that made America the financial and technological powerhouse that it is. The freedom to pursue whatever the hell you want to sets the conditions for creativity and exploration that this nation has benefitted from time and time again. Samuel Colt, Henry Ford, the Wright Brothers, Robert Goddard, Alexander Graham Bell, Jonas Salk...the list of inventors who maximized their potential in a country that allowed them to goes on and on.

Imagine if we had a government that took 75% of everything you made (and yes there are governments that do). Your creativity and ambition would die immediately. You'd never unleash your full potential on the world because all the fruits of your labor would just be confiscated.

The government should take enough to money to provide security and set the conditions for us to succeed (which includes education). A tax free society is a fable and in order to keep our position in the world we all have to give a little, but a government that takes a massive proportion of our wealth and redistributes it in the name of "economic stimulus spending" is really called socialism. How's that working out for North Korea?

So if you really want to accuse the government of inherently un-American behavior, focus your watchful eyes on how much it's taxing you and what it's doing with your money. If people protected their wallets with as much enthusiasm as they protected their holsters we'd have more accountability, less waste, and ultimately more money to do whatever we want with...like buy more guns.

"Are you better off now than you were four years ago?" is a bullshit campaign slogan. It's not the government's job to ensure our fiscal well-being. It's our own. If I choose to spend frivolously and not seek out better employment or a better life then the answer is no, I'm not better off, but is that the government's fault? No matter who is in office life boils down to individual responsibility. Do for yourself what others won't instead of waiting for a handout. Otherwise you're a soccer player taking a dive in the goalie box.

"Where you stand depends on where you sit" is one of the worst anecdotes ever. The notion that a profession drives personal values insinuates that people have no freedom of choice. You have to have the balls to not be ruled by your position. Determine what you believe in and rule your job, not the other way around. Just because you're a Democrat does not mean you have to support welfare. Just because you're a Republican doesn't mean you're pro-life. Just because you're a 7-11 store owner doesn't mean you're any less competent of a businessman than the country club douche you serve.

Some people complain that the government is involved in 'shadow wars' overseas and conspires to topple governments that are unfriendly to ours or at least destabilize them. God I hope so. If not then someone isn't doing his job. Security at home starts with covert operations thousands of miles away. I want our government doing unsavory things overseas so the danger doesn't reach our shores and I don't want to know about it. I just want to know they're doing it. If hooking up a terrorist's brain to a car battery prevents another 9-11 I have two things to say: red is positive, black is negative.

CLASS DIFFERENCES
"Some people regard private enterprise as a predatory tiger to be shot. Others look on it as a cow they can milk. Not enough people see it as a healthy horse, pulling a sturdy wagon."
-Winston Churchill

Ebenezer Scrooge said of society, "There is nothing on which it is so hard as poverty, and yet, there is nothing it condemns with such severity as the pursuit of wealth." Charles Dickens wants you to come to the self-realization that Scrooge is a lonely, shallow, and pitiful cur and we should disdain his petty connection with money as frivolous and damaging. Curmudgeons don't really disagree with the guy's outlook. Sure he could have been less of a dickhead about it, but his opinion is really just a classical view of capitalism. He believes that a successful society with free markets and the ability to dictate your own future necessitates class differences. If you work hard, you get ahead. No handouts. No one there to wipe your ass or give you a free ride. No one to take what you've earned and give it to someone who hasn't done a fucking thing with his life.

Most curmudgeons don't hate the wealthy and in fact it's American to give them a certain amount of respect. A lot of rich people have bad taste and there must be an inversely proportional relationship between an increase in wealth and decrease in overall style, but hating the rich is like hating lobster for being delicious. Most people who took a leap of faith to start their own business and got wealthy doing so have twice the stones as the rest of us. It takes serious guts to leave the security of a fixed income and strike out on your own to produce a product or a service that you think the majority of people in a certain demographic, geographic, or topographic will pay money for. That's what America is all about: opportunity.

If you can sell a piece of plastic that keeps the tags on your Beenie Baby protected and therefore maintains its value and you get rich off of it, then good for you. You spotted an opportunity, used your talent and hard work to produce and market it correctly, and ate your piece of the American pie. Bon appetite. If you gave 50 people jobs or sent fifty thousand dollars worth of business to another company en route to the promised land, then even better. I don't begrudge your success.

The freedom to use your talent to your advantage is America. If people are willing to pay twenty bucks to watch a guy juggle cats, then why should we hate him for it? If LeBron James can use his natural physical talent to play a game and earn forty million dollars a year doing it then good for him. Would we do any differently if we had his abilities? If anyone is to blame for that situation it's us. We're the ones going home after a long day of work and turning on the TV to be entertained by a sporting event or the latest angry cop drama. We're funding them. It's our dollars they're lining their mansions with.

"That he blows on cars and ho's," you might say. Sure, not all athletes are model citizens and many drop stacks of cash on golden showers and underground midget tossing (see my earlier rant on sports), but frivolous materialism is also a rite of passage among that culture. Like politicians, curmudgeons just don't expect anything less than ridiculous behavior from athletes or anyone so we're never disappointed. They always do stupid shit and always will.

Wasteful spending doesn't bother us. Attitude does. The attitude that the wealthy are better than those of us without money is one of the things that keeps curmudgeons angry. The amount of zeros in your checking account doesn't mean you're a better person than those of us content to remain in the middle class. If you're using your money for positive social change then you've earned respect. If you're an idiot getting high and crashing a half-million dollar car into a family then I hope you get a nasty case of rabid herpes during a prison rape. Getting rich isn't a reason to despise someone. Pissing away the gross domestic product of a small nation is. We're proud of you for succeeding and we're equally proud of our country for giving you the opportunity to succeed. Just don't be a douche about it if you can manage it.

If anything we're sympathetic for the wealthy who have had to slice and chop their way to the top only to be rewarded with the crushing loneliness that oftentimes comes with it. Frequently the most successful businessmen are intimately familiar with the unsavory task of fucking someone over and have learned to live with it. Whether they were born that way or compromised who they were to get there doesn't matter. In business you have to plumb the depths of your eternal soul to determine what percent of it is corruptible and still sleep at night. Want to reach stage 3 of Curmudgeonism in a short period of time? Start your own business.

If curmudgeons focus their critical energies on any class of society it's their own. The middle class is the glue. Once they get invested and have something they don't want to lose, they get energized and active in the community, politics, school, you name it. The poor will only fight for what they have and anyone who will provide just a little more. They support whoever pays them or feeds them or convinces them a God wants them to be happy. The middle class is really where the power lies. They're the ones who will determine the fate of any nation and therefore they are the scorn of the curmudgeon more than the wealthy or poor. There's a sense of accountability among peers. We self-correct our own, so just as iron sharpens iron, curmudgeons sharpen curmudgeons in the middle classes.

I (and most middle aged men) don't hate the poor, but we're not willing to let everything we've worked hard for be handed over to someone who hasn't done Jill Schitt either. You can advocate that we all need to pull together and help each other out all day, but what's the point of working hard and building something for my family when someone is just going to come along and take it away? That stifles ingenuity and drive because if you know you're never truly going to get ahead then why try in the first place?

Humans are competitive no matter how you slice up the pie. We want to have more than the next guy and to deny that as a basic human trait is to live in a fantasy world of dungeons and dragons. Now...curmudgeons do not entirely throw up the castle walls and dare you to cross the moats. There are people who deserve a break and good people out there who just need a leg up to be a contributing member of society, so giving those people a helping hand is a benevolent thing. But a handout that leads to more reliance on the state and outright individual laziness? Fuck off.

Anyone who wants a handout instead of earning their way is a poor, miserable creature who will never be independent unless made and kept so by the exertions of better people than themselves. Why do you want a handout in the first place? Why do you want someone to take care of you? The assclowns who call for equality are really just looking for someone to give them something. "We're oppressed and you need to give us more of what you have" is their battle cry.

All humans are entitled to the basic needs: shelter, water, and food in that order and it's right to donate money to help anyone who doesn't have those things, but that's where the line is drawn. Is that selfish and crass? Don't care. Those are my priorities and criteria for helping others. This is where I stand and you won't convince me otherwise.

THE MILITARY

"I'm not worried about the bullet with my name on it. It's the one marked 'to whom it may concern' that scares me."
-Anonymous

I spent 24 years in uniform and have deep opinions on the military and its interaction with society. Some of these opinions may not make sense if you never served in the Armed Forces, so skip ahead if you don't care to read this part, but many of these maxims are also related to life in general.

In any society there are three types of people:

-Prey – Those who have no capacity for violence and

are law-abiding, productive citizens.
-Predator – Those who have a capacity for violence and no empathy for their fellow citizen.
-Protector – Those who have a capacity for violence and a deep love for their fellow citizen; a warrior who walks the virtuous path. These people are rare and to be treasured.

Like many men I decided a long time ago that I was not a predator. I want to not only follow the laws of society but help make it better, so the outlaw gansta life was not for me. But I'm also not prey. I can and will defend myself and my family with extreme prejudice and don't care one bit about inflicting permanent damage to predators. So as a teen I identified with the man who wants to protect the prey from the predators; a sheepdog protecting the flock from the wolf. Everyone should ask himself which one he is.

War may be morally wrong (and I'm not diving into that philosophical trench), but it is an undeniable part of human nature. It's ignorant to build a society that is based on people being the way we have decided they SHOULD be instead of the way they ARE. We cannot wish away conflict. We are not a society of Nevil Chamberlain's and rather than denying the urges, tendencies, and instincts of man, we should seek to channel them into constructive directions. The point is we should never build a society that believes people don't WANT to fight because they always WILL. The goal should be to build a society where the things they fight for are good things.

Where do politics and the military intersect? I believe the government should set the conditions for Americans to succeed and its foreign policy should aim to achieve that goal. Being the world's globo-cop is hypocritical and ultimately inconsistent. We look stupid when we invade Kuwait and kick the Iraqi's out for human rights violations but turn a blind eye to Rwanda. We invaded Afghanistan because we were convinced that the people responsible for 9-11 originated there (and were right), but invaded Iraq by dangling a hollow carrot in front of a mule drunk on nationalistic pride. When our ambassador to Libya was dragged into the streets of Benghazi and executed we should have had a Ranger Battalion on the ground within hours if for no other reason than to tell the world you just can't murder our representatives like that. Fuck with the eagle and you get the talons.

American might should be used to protect American citizens, secure American enterprise, reinforce the American reputation, and kill American enemies. I don't care much for using boots on the ground to ram American values down someone's throat who's only going to throw them back up as soon as we let go, but American might is just that: mighty, and should be used judiciously and our officials should be honest about it. "We're invading Iraq to secure our own economic interests" is a line I can respect more than "we're invading Iraq to eliminate WMD that aren't really there."

Everyone's perception of a measured and appropriate response is different and I think it's important to define what you're willing to fight for at the national level just as much as you do at the individual level. For me it goes like this:

Iraq-Shoulda stayed out.
Former Yugoslavia-Shoulda stayed out more.
Syria-Glad we stayed out.
Rwanda-Why did we stay out?
Somalia-Why did we pull out?
Haiti-Sure, why not?
Benghazi-Get in there and kill.

If I lived in a war zone I'd paint a huge Infrared American flag on my roof to make no mistake who's side I was on. The American military fights at night and we can see everything in the darkness thanks to the power of innovation and the profit motives of Lockheed Martin. You want to keep what meager possessions you have? Make it damn clear whose side you're on. If you're unsure, I'll help you decide: ours.

I don't think the word "winner" is appropriate when referring to someone who was awarded a Medal of Honor, as in "Medal of Honor winner SFC Jones says..." It's not a competition that involves a winner and a loser. Most Medal of Honor acts involve gut-wrenching tales of death and sorrow and I'm betting the brave men who have been awarded one don't feel like they "won" it. I'm also betting every last Medal of Honor recipient would prefer they never got it at all.

The military has a lot of words that are unnecessary, but so cool that we keep them for fear of becoming too modern. Epaulet is one. It's a sublime holdover from the chivalric age when we cared about all the dangly things on our uniforms. You have to look epaulet up to realize it's a shoulder board and even then it means nothing.

"Motherfucker" is a standard unit of measure in the military that I hope never goes away. Anything can be as long / heavy / far / or stupid as a motherfucker and every soldier knows exactly what that unit of measure is. No explanation necessary. Anything can be long as fuck, strong as fuck, heavy as fuck, steady as fuck, bad as fuck, and even shitty as fuck. The military paved the way for perverting every bodily part and process into a derogatory term and has the most versatile uses for every cuss word. What's better is they're allowed and even expected to be used in the workplace. If you don't have the mouth of a soldier then you're not one.

LEADERSHIP
"Leadership is the art of getting someone else to do something you want done because he wants to do it."
-Dwight D. Eisenhower

Everyone respects a great leader. We're drawn to them because they make our lives better and no one worth a plug nickel wants to follow a turd. Before falling in line behind a Pied Piper and pledging your loyalty to him or her, be on the lookout for certain attributes.

Be consistent

If a leader punishes someone for an offense then he can't let another person off the hook for the same infraction unless he wants an active insurrection in the ranks. I knew a Brigade Commander who had a favorite Captain. One day the golden boy got drunk and took a swing at a Major. It was clearly a violation of the Uniform Code of Military Justice as well as thoroughly embarrassing since he missed the Major's chin completely. No matter how much the Commander liked this guy he knew he had to throw the book at him or it would have sent a message to the rest of the Brigade-as long as you're one of my boys, you're untouchable. That's Cosa Nostra leadership, not US military. The standards are the same from the lowest member of the totem pole to the highest, so you have to be consistent in every aspect.

But don't have absolutes

Don't confuse consistency with absolutes. When I took command of a company I said, "Anyone who gets a DUI is toast. No questions asked." That was stupid. Halfway through command I had a troop get a DUI, but there were extenuating circumstances. He got drunk and then got in his car and went to sleep in the back seat because he knew driving was a bad idea. Great judgment call on his part, but since it was December he put the keys in the ignition to get warm before falling asleep. When a cop found him, he was charged with DUI because in the state of Georgia keys in the ignition is enough to charge the driver. He was a great soldier with a distinguished career and was one of the most trustworthy guys I ever knew. My statement that I would punish anyone who got a DUI proved to be an albatross around my neck and put me in a bad position. I had to go easy on him and learned that every situation is different and having an absolute stance on anything is about as smart as not wearing a condom in a Haitian brothel.

It's not a popularity contest

Being responsible means you have to be an asshole sometimes. This can also be worded as, "NEVER make a decision because it's popular."
Example: After a Field Training Exercise my Battalion had all our weapons turned in to the arms room except one, the Battalion Commander's driver, who was on the road ferrying the old man around. The whole Battalion waited and waited for this guy to bring his weapon in so we could be released for the night. Those are two hours of my life I will never recover. As the second in command I could have sent all of the troops home and been the cool guy, but it was against our procedures to release anyone until every weapon was accounted for. So we waited while I lit up every cell phone and radio net in the state to get Corporal

Dumbass to bring his weapon to the arms room. Don't succumb to peer pressure and make a decision to look cool. If I cared about being popular, I wouldn't have written this book.

A zero defect mentality is for zeroes

Throughout the 1990's, when the Army was mostly in garrison for years at a time and we had little to do but train, a pervasive attitude of "zero defects" emerged. If everything wasn't perfect, then you were a shitbag. This was especially true at the company commander level because we had to report statistics like reenlistment, physical fitness, weapons qualifications, maintenance, exorcisms performed, blah blah blah. If the Battalion Commander saw one statistic from your company that was less than perfect, then your command ended prematurely and you were assigned to a radar station in Alaska.

It was stupid and we finally came around to realize that things break and shit happens. Having perfect stats only meant you were hiding something or fudging the numbers. It's okay to step on your dick, just don't march on it. It's simply unrealistic to expect people to be perfect. Instead, expect them to attack a leadership crisis with vigor and moxie and be creative or experienced enough to come up with a solution.

When Private Snuffy sets his barracks room on fire, does Sergeant Smuckatelli handle it professionally or does he sit on his ass and throw a coat of paint on it? When Corporal Jones can't figure out how to clear a weapon jam, does his Squad Leader show him how to shoot correctly or ignore him? Subordinate leaders must be willing and able to deal with issues quickly and efficiently instead of expecting them to never happen.

The same is true of those appointed over you. In an office setting, a supervisor has the responsibility of handling a crisis to the best of his abilities instead of walking away or sweeping it under the rug. Those who dodge a bullet only to have it hit one of their workers is a cowardly failure. Curmudgeons have no stomach for that type of person, but...

Don't be insubordinate

We may be surly, but when a decision is made by someone with more authority than us, we support it even when we don't want to. It doesn't do any good to do otherwise. No matter how stupid a command decision might seem, you are bound to follow it and not be an insubordinate jackass. If your boss orders everyone to get qualified as tugboat captains then grab a bright orange life vest and find your sea legs. Support it and deal with it. The last thing you should do is announce your displeasure over a command decision to your co-workers.

Bitch in private and praise in public

This one is tricky for curmudgeons. In my twenties and thirties I had a professional demeanor and discretion, but the older I get the less I care about that. Still, embarrassing someone for pleasure is a dick move unless he or she truly deserves it. Some people think it's an effective learning tool to thoroughly embarrass a person in front of his peers in order to get him to change his negative behavior. Those people swear Tupac is still alive and think sex can last more than eight minutes (fucking crazy talk!). Usually, all it does is ostracize the problem child from the rest of his team. Don't get me wrong, people who need an attitude adjustment should get one from a supervisor named Spartacus who has prior convictions and mommy issues, but the best place to do that is normally behind closed doors. Likewise anyone who deserves a pat on the

back should get it in front of his peers as publicly as
possible.

FAMILY
"Some people never go crazy.
What truly horrible lives they must lead."
-Charles Bukowski

Half the world's problems can be solved through
good parenting. If you give a crap about your kid then you
can help them become a great adult who in turn makes
society better. If you think they're just a nuisance and don't
deserve your time, then they'll turn out to be criminals or
crack whores and burden the rest of us. Congrats on raising
one.

Never forget that kids are a direct reflection of
their parents. When we tell them to do something or not do
something it's because those are our values that we're
trying to instill in them. Hold a door for a lady, put your
napkin in your lap, work hard and do the right thing even
when no one is looking...these are values parents believe
and we pass those beliefs along to our children. If you think
otherwise then either you're trying hard to make them into
something you're not or you've lost perspective on life. If a
kid is successful then it's a good bet his folks gave him the
tools he needed to get there. If he's a little asshole then his
parents probably are too.

When a kid fails, a parent fails even if they can't
admit it. Yes, there are a lot of variables that the parents
can't always control, but we all shape our kids to be like us,
so when they steal something, kill an animal, or get an F
we're left wondering why, when we should stare into the
mirror and the family photo albums and try to identify what
we could have done differently. At least the parents that
give a shit do. The ones who don't end up saying, "Little

Johnny couldn't have done this awful thing you're accusing him of" even in the face of mountains of evidence. Those are the delusional ones.

Sure this is a generalization, but it passes the duck test eight times out of ten (if it looks like a duck and walks like a duck and quacks like a duck then don't call it a fucking goose). Kids need attention and have to be raised right and that doesn't always mean in the way *you* think is right, but someone who has been proven to raise great kids, like Eisenhower's parents, thinks is right. If you doubt your ability as a parent then forget trying to mold them in your image. Mold them in the image of someone who made a difference. Being a parent is permanent. There aren't any do-overs, so stick it out to the end and do your best no matter how badly you want to quit or take a day off. When you earn the title of 'father' you don't get a vacation.

The moment you realize your parents weren't full of shit sucks because you wanted so badly to hate them and now you can't. When you become a parent and see they went through the same difficulties that you're going through there's a level of respect (or at the very least understanding) that maybe they were just confused young adults trying to figure out diapers, crying, formula, training wheels, budgets, Amazon.com, and all the other little things you're struggling with. Kids will never respect their parents until they endure the same hardships and realize that mom and dad might not have been idiots after all.

Kids always say parents don't understand them. The truth is parents have a hard time understanding all the environmental factors their kids are being subjected to. I'm talking about technology. We understand their feelings and emotions and the core of what they're going through, but we don't really fathom the differences new technology brings into the equation. Our parents only had to deal with the impacts of movies, music, and the hideousness of MTV. In our day we didn't have social media or smartphones and all the vile new ways kids can get into trouble with them like cyber bullying.

It's hard for us to understand why a kid should care what another kid says on Facebook. Hateful comments are just digits on a screen. We don't get it, yet kids kill themselves every day across America because of what other kids say about them on a dumb ass social website. It's sickening and the most awful aspect is that it makes us lose faith for both the bully and the bullied. You harassed a kid until he committed suicide? You're a piece of shit. You killed yourself because of what someone else thought? You're weak and selfish. And I can say that. I've been to the edge of that abyss and offered myself to whatever God lurked in its deep dark depths, but he didn't want me.

Children frequently mistake their parent's silence for stupidity. They think parents don't respond to an event because they don't know any better when in fact parents know the value of discretion and the importance of letting them be wrong. We don't feel the need to respond to everything they say because they're just going to disagree and start an argument, so we let asinine things like, "we should just surrender to the Russians to avoid a nuclear war" go. They tell themselves that our silence is complicity, but the truth is we just don't want to fight with them over banal crap and sometimes the experience of falling on your face is just as formative as success. Failure can be the best teacher.

Adult impatience will make weak kids. Their arguing grates on our nerves so we step in to mediate a truce, but we're really just making them dependent. The problem lies in the subconscious precedent. They're unknowingly getting used to someone settling their quarrels for them so when they're teenagers and young adults embroiled in a confrontation with a peer, they look around for someone to step in and end it for them. They become dependent on others and not strong enough to stand up for themselves and it's our fault for not being more patient. When the kids are arguing, let them work it out themselves no matter how much it sucks to listen to it.

Curmudgeons are overprotective, especially with family members; a trait that stems from our trust issues. It's not like kidnapping and molesting kids are new things. They've been around forever, but the mass media that brings information to us at light speed makes sure we all know the second a sordid neighbor has abducted, raped, and killed a child. It contributes to us being overbearing overlords when it comes to their safety.

When I was eight years old I rode my bicycle around our Virginia neighborhood for hours and hours a day with no regard for any parental supervision. By ten, I was walking two miles to the local Stop and Rob to get milk for the family with no cares in the world. Did anyone watch me? Nope. Will I let my kids do that today? No fucking way. Why? Because 20/20 and Dateline have convinced me the moment I let them out of my site they'll meet a horrifying end. The news is like *Jaws*, convincing us not to stick our toes in the water lest we lose our lives.

There's a very delicate balance between being overprotective and underprotective with kids. Too overprotective and they grow up wanting to take stupid risks just to piss you off (which could kill them). Too under protective and they do stupid shit because they don't know the risks (which could also kill them). It's quite possibly the most delicate line in the world since good or bad parenting makes all the difference in a life. No pressure, dad.

Having kids has made me look at everything like it's alive because of those damn cartoons and movies with living inanimate objects like *Planes* and *Cars*. At any moment I expect toys to spring to life and start singing show tunes. Throwing away my toothbrush feels like murder. I took my dishwasher to the dump and swear it cried as I left.

I want my kids to see me drink and be in control because I want them to learn this is what normal and acceptable alcohol consumption looks like. Throwing back a few cocktails and calmly watching TV or having dinner with no noticeable behavioral changes is what they should think is the right way to drink. Slurring, puking, and confessing your sins are undisciplined and amateurish. If you can't hold your liquor then switch to poker.

Parents wonder why they have fewer friends after having children. News flash: life as you knew it is over. Your life gets consumed by puke, diapers, music lessons, practices, driving, and proms and there's no time for your own socializing. By the time you come up for air, your friends are bald and fat and so are you and you're left wondering what happened to those smooth chiseled bodies you and your wife had and why you're too tired to put out the effort to get back to that state. You measure your life in the accomplishments or failures of your kids, not your own anymore.

It physically hurts when something you've paid for gets broken. You don't see the accidental droppage. You don't see the mistake or lack of attention someone wasn't paying at the moment of breakage. All you see is the money you worked hard to earn being wasted. A kid drops an iPad and cracks the glass on one corner. It still works and yes, it was an accident, but it's like watching someone break your fingers. You worked hard to evolve those digits and spent lots of time learning how to use them properly, putting each piece of finely cut cheese into your mouth while trying to grasp the nuances of how each knuckle worked in painstaking detail. You mastered the technique of the jump shot in junior high. You learned to type in high school and had deep reverence for the exquisite engineering of fingers when they invaded the deep recesses of Mary Jane Rottencrotch's scintillating pretty pink panties in the back of a 1968 Charger. You would rather chew on aluminum foil than watch them be damaged and are incensed at the notion of such a fine system of genetics cast aside like trash. So why is it so easy to pass off a physical object that you worked so hard to afford being broken in front of you as "an acceptable accident?"

It comes down to standards. If you work at a job for X number of hours on any given day or week to afford a necessary item or a luxury that you want to spend your paycheck on, then breaking it is an offense. It's a declaration that you don't give a shit about my labor and are okay with casting the fruits of my sweat aside carelessly. In that case, I say get a job and buy it yourself. You're only 10 years old? Tough shit.

There's a fine line between pride and revulsion when you catch your son hiding under his bedspread and begging you to leave his room. If you've ever had to crack a bedsheet open before throwing it in the washer then you know the stomach turning sickness that comes with it, but there's little to do but accept it as the natural course of things. Kids eventually explore their sexuality and once they learn how things work they go hog wild with their own genitals, right? And after all...has any man escaped being discovered by a parent in a compromising position? If your answer is yes then I'll say you didn't live much as a teen and need to make up for it now. Get thee to a strip bar!

It's ironic how we tell kids to be quiet and eat their dinner when they're young, but once they hit puberty, we beg them to say anything at all. Instead we just get a cold stare from underneath jet black Emo hair and a terse, "I don't want to eat. I think I'll go to my room, turn out the lights, and listen to The Cure."

The same can be true of when they want something and don't want to work for it.
Example:
"Dad...can you open this candy wrapper?"
"No."
"But dad...it's too tight for me."
"If you want to eat that candy badly enough, you'll find a way to open it."

The kid will cry and you'll hate it so much that for the next ten minutes you'll doubt yourself and want to rush over, open it, and say, "There! It's not so hard is it?" But if you wait and give him a chance to succeed then and the crying will stop, he'll find a knife and slit that bad boy open like a freshly bagged deer.

Some young people strive to be the opposite of what their parents expect them to be just to spite them. But then they follow through and achieve that goal and end up hanging their head in shame when they realize how damaging that hate can be.

KNOW YOURSELF
"Don't be so smug about your morality when it's never been tested."
-Anonymous

Being a curmudgeon is all about knowing who you are and what you're capable of. You must know how far you can go and when to stop. It is the great fallacy of many that they continue to think their minds and bodies are capable of doing the things they did in their prime. They lack honest friends, mirrors, stopwatches, or anything that provides unbiased truth in their lives. This is where curmudgeons can be helpful. We provide the perspective that so many people need. It's easy to blame the people pointing fingers at you, but hard to figure out why they're doing it.

Dreamers say "You can achieve anything if you just put your mind to it." Poppycock. I can put my mind to being on the US Olympic rugby team 24/7 and will never achieve it because the cold truth is there are people with truckloads more athletic skill than me who are half as fragile now that I'm in middle age. There are things that are simply not possible because they violate the laws of physics and probability so those who say you can achieve anything are the same people who believe Congressmen are motivated by the will of the people.

Challenging yourself is great, but there are things that cross the divide between adrenaline and stupidity. Riding a bull? No thanks. Downhill skiing? Catch an edge and you're fucked. Cliff diving…misjudge the tide and you're bird shit on a rock. Bowling a 300? Now that sounds perfectly Spartan.

You have to know when you're simply making a fool of yourself and stop. One drink into the evening I feel horny, two drinks in I want to fight. After three I'm a Viking and four I'm Eisenhower driving 5 million Americans across Europe to decimate the hideous Nazi horde. But then things change somewhere in the middle of the fifth cocktail. I'm suddenly sitting on the couch willing to watch The Real Housewives of Anywhere and if I make it to a sixth drink then a coma isn't too far behind. Sex? No thanks. I'll just have a Metamucil and go to bed no matter how badly anyone ridicules me.

Incidentally it's comforting to know inhibitions melt away with an intake of alcohol no matter what your age. Even at 45 a few drinks into the evening you want to conquer the world. You'd think we'd outgrow this phenomenon with age, but we don't and maybe that's a good thing. It's something we can point to from our youth that is still the same now as it was then.

CURMUDGEON SOUND BYTES
Too short to be maxims, too long to be quotes

"It's been my pleasure to serve you," is such a lie. Pleasure is a beach, a sip of bourbon, or an orgasm. So unless you're drunk, have sand in your toes, or just came in your pants, then serving me a cheeseburger is not a pleasure. And if it is I'm not coming back here, so save us both the indignity of lying and just say, "hope you enjoy it." That I can believe.

Being a businessman is like chasing fireflies on a moonless night. Every time you grab for one it either moves away or you open your hand and nothing's there. But once in a while you get lucky and catch one, which makes you want to keep chasing, so you devise new ways to succeed. It's an insidious cycle of perseverance, adulation, and creativity.

Don't let storytellers off easy. Make them take the extra effort to be convincing or walk away. There's nothing worse than people who tell a tale for ten minutes with no punch line. If you're going to take up part of my life to tell me a story then it has to be interesting. What's the point? What's the meaning? Why am I standing here listening to you when I could be watching the Discovery Channel?

Some people stand on a beach or stare at an iconic view waiting for an epiphany to show them what they've done right or wrong in their lives and illuminate which path they should follow next. Curmudgeons stand on a mountain and see a beautiful view, maybe even feel small compared to the wonderful world, but as for hearing the voice of God whisper some divine secret of the meaning of life or have a double-rainbow-youtubegasm, that just never happens. We have to physically feel something to know its meaning. It has to kick us in the face or knock the wind out of us or it's not real. If God spoke to me about the meaning of life, I would probably consider myself schizophrenic or write it off as a Monty Python flashback.

Some peacenik schmuck will say, "if we can just get 33 million people to hold hands on the equator we can end war," but in reality you'll just drown 16 million because they'll be in the oceans. Don't they know basic geography?

People say "take it easy" all the time and there are magazine articles and TV specials on men who live to be 110 by never stressing over anything. Stress is good for those who enjoy productivity. It forces us to get shit done. Stress away.

Why does every shooting spree have to be in places where good people work or go to school? Why can't it be in a prison or an Al Qaeda training camp?

Sometimes when you get a stupid question, you have to answer with exactly what the person wants to hear even if there's no truth to it just so they'll go the fuck away.

There are some phrases that I don't want to know the origin of. "The Whole Nine Yards" – I know where that comes from and it's a pretty cool story. "Waxing the Bishop" – don't care to know.

I hear some people say exclusion is a bad thing; that everyone needs to have access to everything and there should be no such thing as cliques or groups or off limits areas. Get real. There's something alluring about being on the other side of the red velvet rope and a satisfaction that comes with earning the right to be there. People who think humans don't like exclusion need only look at the difference between Facebook and myspace.

Little is surprising in America when it comes to opulence. We've cornered the market on luxury, but getting hot water that's instantly hot without waiting for it to warm up is mind blowing.

Curmudgeons are by definition middle aged. We don't have epic nights anymore, so when you have the chance to run victory laps around your buddy because he puked first, take it. It's rare past 30.

Distance is a girl's best friend. From 200 meters a chick can be a 10. At 100 meters she gets downgraded to an 8. At 10 meters she's a 4 and we're looking back at the 200 meter targets wondering where the hot chick disappeared to.

Rent is one of the worst concepts in human evolution. When someone rents something they don't give a shit about its condition but when they own it they take care of it. Force people to buy an apartment, condo, house, whatever and they'll take care of it and make it theirs because they're invested. Ownership brings about change at the grassroots level. The only thing that should ever be rented is porn.

If someone wants to kill another person badly enough, he'll find anything capable of doing the job: a golf club, a rabid alligator, a candlestick in the library. So don't blame the tool. Blame the person wielding it. A dude was killed with a hammer last week. Should we ban them? Let's make construction workers use rocks instead? Oh wait...we used to stone people to death. Shit!

Learning that a homicide was an inside job takes a little bit of the edge off. An unstable family member with access to weapons taking out his frustrations on his family isn't nearly as rattling as a random act of violence like someone knocking on a door and killing whomever answers it. That shit can happen anywhere and forces the overprotective people to reevaluate household defense plans.

Some people advocate private ownership of automatic weapons because they fear government. I fear a government outgunned by the people.

There's a difference between a risk and a gamble. A risk you can recover from when it goes bad. A gamble you can't.
Example:
Driving a car is a risk because there are always variables you can't control, but in the end you're driving your own car and can influence the outcome of an unanticipated event because you're in the driver's seat and in control of your faculties. Flying is a gamble. If something goes wrong it's often catastrophic and you have no control over the outcome. If you get into an uncontrollable situation then kiss your ass goodbye.

You know you're dead when there's a scorching hot chick next to you on a plane. I always get stuck next to the snoring, invasive, smelly shitbird when I fly, so I'm convinced the first time I'm seated next to Sophia Vergara we're going down (like she flies coach...Pshaw!). It's either nature's way of letting me die with one last glimpse of the beauty it's capable of making, the universe's way of reminding me who's in charge, or God's way of saying "If you'd loved me more you could have had this." How spiteful.

Silence is golden. Don't ruin it with idle chit chat about your pets, the weather, or pre-menstrual cramping.
Curmudgeons don't mind the awkward silence of a car, a bank line, or urinal. We're confident in who we are and don't have any desire to talk just for the sake of talking or listen just for the sake of listening. When you feel the urge

to make small talk, go find someone who gives a shit cause we don't.

Male priorities are easy to map out over time:
Toys toys toys school girls toys muscles girls kissing muscles boobs boobs cars muscles sex sex sex drink sex sex sex drink drink sex music sex sex drink fight puke work sex sex sex sex sex sex sex sex sex work sex kids sex sex sex kids sex kids drink work work work kids work kids sleep sleep kids sex sleep kids bitch sleep kids bitch bitch bitch Viagra sex bitch bitch bitch Viagra sex heartattack nap bitch bitch bitch nap darkness.

Frugality is fine, but there's nothing wrong with spending a little money on the things that matter like a bed, a house, or a good watch. If you're going to stare at an object that reminds you of your mortality several times a day or lay your head down on an object to rest then they may as well be exquisite things.

I would prefer to be impotent than to find the perfect house that's just beyond my budget. Either way I feel inadequate. A soft dick I can compensate for with a hard tongue, but I can't overcome a lack of income. The end result of sex is momentary pleasure while the end result of a new house is permanent comfort.

Tough should never be used to describe a person unless it refers to his skin. Tough is for cow products. Beef jerky is tough. Leather is tough. Men are resilient, highly trained, or badass, but not tough.

"Everyone deserves a second chance" is bullshit. There are worthless people in this world who do horrific things and deserve absolutely nothing but a painful death. Don't feel bad about not giving someone a second chance if they don't deserve it.

Wealthy people produce one of two things: squared away, motivated kids who want to follow in their footsteps and work hard or spoiled brats who have no idea how life works and don't care to try because they've been handed everything. There's rarely a middle ground.

I want a guy named Dick next to me in a barfight. With that name he's probably spent a lifetime getting picked on and standing up for himself, so there's a good chance he's a trained pugilist and has your back. Forget all the Mikes and Johns of the world. When the shit hits the fan I want a Dick behind me.

When you're under 20 using the excuse "because I want to" is selfish and pretentious because you haven't earned the right to be that way. But over 40 it's a perfectly valid reason to do whatever you fancy and those 20 year-olds can kiss your ass.

I don't want to read a book by anyone under the age of thirty. It's not that I don't think they can write or they don't have anything interesting to say. But the likelihood that they're going to teach me anything is the same as Paris Hilton's tears curing Ebola.

Every man is flawed. We all have those little annoying things that aren't quite right with us. Women just need to ask themselves how many flaws they can live with and still lead a happy, tolerant life because the chances of finding a flawless man are the same as finding a unicorn that can play poker, which is ridiculous since they have hooves. I mean how would they hold the cards?

Likewise, men should accept women's drawbacks. They're just as flawed as us and drive us batshit crazy, but that's okay. If life were perfect we wouldn't need country music.

One-uppers deserve public humiliation. Turning the conversation into something about you is like putting ketchup on steak. It's tasteless and provides an opportunity to put someone who desperately needs it in his or her place. I don't care if your semen cures Alzheimer's, there's no lower slimeball than someone who steals the spotlight (especially in a social setting) from someone else who rightfully deserves it. Go back to middle school and gossip about which one of your clique figured out who shot JR first.

Maybe people never really have as much in common as we think we do, but the differences are invisible in our youth. When you're a kid, you're a kid; interested in the same thing every kid is interested in: having fun. As we grow older we mature and branch out into the things we love to do and leave the other kids behind. So even though Dave, Mike, Tim, and I were tight in our teens and twenties doesn't automatically make it so for our thirties and beyond. Dave's unwavering faith, Tim's ambition, and Mike's liberalism weren't on the driveway basketball courts we played on, but those characteristics dominate them now and we're not nearly as compatible as we were back then. My curmudgeonism doesn't exactly help, but you know what? They're still my brothers.

Social media is like fishing.
The cast: *Sigh.* Not feeling great today.
The nibble: What's wrong, Peaches?
Teasing the fish: It's Sean.
Setting the hook: What happened?

The reel in: Well, I thought he was acting weird. We had plans to meet at a nice place for dinner but he was so quiet. Conversation wasn't flowing. I asked him what was wrong. He said "nothing" in that 'there's something wrong but I don't want to tell you' way. I told him I loved him but he just smiled and kept eating. We drove home in silence and watched TV and now I feel as if I've lost him completely. I went to bed hoping he'd come in and want sex, but he just fell asleep without saying anything. I sobbed and then cried when I heard him snoring. I hate this. I want to leave. I want to scream. I want to eat out of emotion and drink until I slap him in the face! I may leave him.
Meanwhile Sean is thinking, "Missed a record buck by inches. Can't figure out how."

There's nothing wrong with deleting unimportant information from your brain's hard drive. Especially names. "Sean is in Colin's class this year," my wife says as I nod like a pitcher accepting a call from the catcher with no intent of throwing what he asked for. In reality I'm thinking, *Who's Sean? Is he pimply kid, freckle kid, or the one who keeps dismantling the decorative stone wall in front of my plant beds? Why do I care?* Names just don't stick with curmudgeons, which is why the Indian naming system seems so much more efficient. "Killed a Coyote," 'Big Gap Tooth," or 'Never Gets Laid" would stick with a person forever. Of course I'd most likely be "Confused Bald White Man" or "Smells Like Fire Water."

Nothing shuts a party down like saying something no one has the guts to argue about like "I think teachers should be armed." It's not that I believe it, but it provides a few brief moments of confused silence before the rage begins. Then walk away. You can't win that argument.

There's something about a guitar that makes me want to leave a party immediately. It's like the Pied Piper in reverse.

Being on the verge of a big deal is worse than losing it. I can deal with disappointment, but hope drives me crazy.

All my life I wanted a cool car and just about the time I could afford one I discovered these things called implants. Now my wife is my car cause I take the top off and ride that ass.

Breast implants are like eBooks. You get what all the fuss is about, but you still like the feel of the original.

There's a big difference between a helping hand and a handout. One leads to independence and the other laziness.

When I go to an amusement park I'm convinced there is a shortage of mirrors in the world.

I'm never more impressed by the human body as I am on the day after Thanksgiving when I witness firsthand how much a colon can store.

You know you've made it when you have the word "Supreme" in your job title. The Supreme Allied Commander Europe is a badass moniker.

My meds have a warning label. "May cause dizziness. Alcohol will intensify this effect."
Get my shot glasses, son.

True friends are the ones you hang out with for 2 hours and it never occurs to you to check your Facebook status.

Never associate with someone so uncreative that he names his Chocolate Labrador 'Hershey.'

Dear Musicians, If I wanted to hear ooooh oooooh yeah yeah yeah, I'd watch a porno. Be more creative.

Vanity plates are a sad, lonely cry for attention unless you use them to deliver a meaningful message. Mine says HATEPPL.

People who walk down the street muttering incomprehensible dribble; who are they taking to? Wait...who am I?

A sense of humor is directly proportional to income. When I'm making money I'm Mister Slapstick but when I'm broke I'm just an angry dick.

There is a direct and proportional relationship between my wife's menstrual cycle and the length of my showers.

If you think your physical prowess is indefinite, you will have a hard landing when your body fails you.

I want to explore genealogy.com but I'm terrified that it will reveal my wife is really my cousin. Then sex will be awkward.

Short fries and small chips keep people honest. They eliminate the possibility of double dipping.

I love fish. Especially the black kind with four legs that goes "moo."

There are some people you can train, teach, and buy books for, but all they'll do is eat the covers.

No one in this world is more talented at separating a man from his money than Walt Disney.

I tried golf but had a hard time playing a game where your goal is to shoot an eagle and success is measured in how many times you stroke your ball.

Golf is an unsatisfying sport. When I shoot birdies I don't want it to result in a number on a scorecard. I want dinner.

There are two sides to every story. Just because you claim the sky is falling does not mean the clouds don't have a perfectly good explanation for losing altitude.

There are much greater foes in this world than I. Time and gravity rarely lose a fight.

I'm convinced that I'm going to hell, so I'd like to live a long life to delay the journey.

If I wear Bermuda shorts then I can drink on Bermuda time.

I have heard of this sobriety tribe that you speak of. I cannot imagine they have the gumption for a fight.

Five o'clock is a finish line and booze is my trophy.

Self-confidence is a lesion on the liver of truth that grows stronger every time I drink. Because the more I drink the bigger and badder I get.

Men don't turn to idiots when we drink. We're already idiots. The drink just removes our camouflage.

I do not take comfort in talking to gravestones. The people I knew talked back.

It's hard to keep a tapestry of lies straight, which is why I never learned to weave.

Being homeless must be boring. Except for that whole survival thing.

Moving day is like watching a house vomit.

Being healthy can be a curse. You're the one who has to bury all the friends and the family who made bad choices.

Yes, I know you didn't expect me to act this way, son. But it's my job to embarrass you and I take that responsibility very seriously.

Life is like rugby. When the ball comes to you, you have two choices-take the hard road and charge into a line of large men with bad intentions or take the easy way out and pass the ball to someone else who's willing to try.

Candy jars should be banned in the workplace. What good can possibly come from handing out free candy to your employees unless they're secretly concentrated 5-Hour Energy drops wrapped in a candy shell of Vivarin.

Want to stop traffic? Pull over, put on a gas mask and walk around your car like you're looking for something. Everyone...and I mean EVERYONE...will gawk and/or panic until traffic completely stops eight seconds later.

For most middle aged men, the desire to be vulnerable, to temporary lose control in order to prove that you can regain it is there, just below the surface. It's a guilty pleasure that reinforces who we are.

We don't understand how humans truly work until it's too late. As we age we see what really motivates people to do what they do and we see the patterns, but by then we're too old to take any action on it. Therefore the fortunate ones are those who can figure it out early and use it to their advantage.

Those who believe in internet activism also believe in prayer. Neither is a viable course of action. Action is action. Prayer and hashtags are hopes. Hope is not a plan.

Husband: What is that?
Wife: A Keepsake
Husband: What's a keepsake?
Wife: Something I don't use anymore but I don't have the heart to get rid of.
Husband: So you're my keepsake?

This is the greatest lesson my son
And I know it to be true
Don't rely on anyone
They'll only disappoint you

CURMUDGEON QUOTES

I hate cliché quotes and don't advocate using them. If you're going to pick a favorite quote and throw it around at a bar or neighborhood pool parties, don't use something familiar like "Fortune favors the bold." Switch it up and make your own quote to get the point across like "God buttfucks cowards who don't go off the high dive!"

It's disappointing that so many curmudgeonly quotes come from Europeans like Kipling, Churchill, and George Bernard Shaw, but that's the way it is. They've enjoyed a long head start on curmudeonism over North America and have a very good perspective on surliness after so many wars, plagues, genocides, financial collapses, and social experiments gone awry. We have great sourpusses like WC Fields, Henry Louis Mencken, Oscar Wilde and Hunter S. Thompson who was old-school cool. These are my favorites. Find your own pied piper and give the man credit.

"Some scientists claim that hydrogen, because it is so plentiful, is the basic building block of the universe. I dispute that. I say there is more stupidity than hydrogen, and that is the basic building block of the universe."
-Frank Zappa

"Whatever your opinion is on prostitution, at least the customer comes first."
-Paul Leitner-Wise

"There's nothing more confident than a toothless whore."
-Tammy Pescatelli

"Control is an illusion. The sun never asks us if it can rise. Death takes us all and does not your scrotum need kicking? It's nearly impossible to do that by yourself."

-*Stephen Colonna*

"Coffee is not a culture. It's a beverage."
-*Anthony Bourdain*

"Fools take a knife and stab people in the back. The wise take the knife, cut the cord, and set themselves free from the fools."
-*Rachel Woolchin*

"When a man opens a car door for his wife, it's either a new car or a new wife."
-*Prince Philip*

"Wood burns faster when you have to cut and chop it yourself."
-*Harrison Ford*

"The best cure for sea sickness is to sit under a tree."
-*Spike Milligan*

"Lawyers believe a man is innocent until proven broke."
-*Robin Hall*

"Kill one man and you're a murderer, kill a million and you're a conqueror."
-*Jean Rostand*

"We are here on earth to do good unto others. What the others are here for, I have no idea."
-*WH Auden*

"I don't believe in astrology. I am a Sagittarius and we're very skeptical."
-*Arthur C. Clarke*

I don't need friends. I have Amazon.
-*John Ogden*

"Hope is what the world would look like if our dreams came true."
-*Arthur Golden*

"The first piece of luggage on the carousel never belongs to anyone."
-*George Roberts*

"If God had intended us to fly he would have made it easier to get to the airport."
-*Jonathan Winters*

"Compromise and tolerance are magic words. It took me 40 years to become philosophical."
-*Hedy Lamar*

"There is an inverse relationship between reliance on the state and self-reliance."
-*William F. Buckley Jr.*

"I have certainly seen more men destroyed by the desire to have a wife and child and to keep them in comfort than I have seen destroyed by drink and harlots."
-*William Butler Yeats*

"There are certain wicked people in the world that you can't deal with except by force."
-*John Keegan*

"Never interrupt a man when he is busy making mistakes."
-*Napoleon*

"It takes a very shallow knowledge of history to think that there are solutions to most problems."
-*Robert Kaplan*

"A man's wife is his compromise with the illusion of his first sweetheart."
-*George Jean Nathan*

"There is something pagan in me that I cannot shake off. In short, I deny nothing, but doubt everything."
-*Lord Byron*

"The easiest way to be cheated is to believe yourself to be more cunning than others."
-*Pierre Charron*

"The maximum effective range of an excuse is zero."
-*Old Army anecdote*

"It takes years to build trust but only suspicion, not proof, to destroy it."
-*Mr. Green (@iGreenMonk)*

"Those who can, lead. Those who can't, teach."
-*Old Army anecdote*

"A speech should be like a mini-skirt, long enough to cover the subject, but short enough to keep it interesting."
–*Unknown*

Louis CK
"Every day starts, my eyes open and I reload the program of misery. I open my eyes, remember who I am, what I'm like, and I just go, 'Ugh'."

"I'm bored is a useless thing to say. You live in a great big vast world that you've seen none percent of."

"I don't stop eating when I'm full. The meal isn't over when I'm full. It's over when I hate myself."

Lewis Black
"I wake up in the morning and I think everything's going to be great. I'm really kind of optimistic, and I look forward to a new day. I pick up 'The New York Times,' and I look at the front page and realize that once again I'm wrong."

"I'm a happy person but an angry citizen."

"If you're going to vote for somebody because you think they have a great faith in God, you'd better be sure that God has faith in them."

"The thing that makes my generation The Greatest is our ability to hang out. We're spectacular at it. If you take somebody from my generation and sit them on a couch and bring them food and plumbing, they'll sit there and talk to you about anything you want until the day you die."

"There is absolutely nothing you can learn out of one bloodshot eye."

"Usually I'm too tired to apologize."

"A lot of people want to be assistants to celebrities. If you're pursuing that, you're an idiot. You're a moron. The shortest distance between two points is not a celebrity, or being next to a celebrity."

"A guy joins the military because he needs discipline and has to find himself. But don't tell me, 'Golf helps you find yourself.' I've been playing my whole life, and I'm still looking for myself."

W.C. Fields
"Start every day off with a smile and get it over with."

"If you can't dazzle them with brilliance, baffle them with bull."

Henry Louis Mencken
"Marriage is a wonderful institution. But who would want to live in an institution?"

"I simply can't imagine competence as anything save admirable, for it is very rare in this world, and especially in this great Republic, and those who have it in some measure, in any art or craft from adultery to zoology, are the only human being I can think of who will be worth the oil it will take to fry them in Hell."

George Bernard Shaw
"Silence is the most perfect expression of scorn."

"People who say it cannot be done should not interrupt those who are doing it."

"Beware of false knowledge; it is more dangerous than ignorance."

"The moment we want to believe something, we suddenly see all the arguments for it, and become blind to the arguments against it."

"The power of accurate observation is commonly called cynicism by those who have not got it."

"Alcohol is the anesthesia by which we endure the operation of life."

"Every man over forty is a scoundrel."

Hunter S Thompson
"If you're going to be crazy, you have to get paid for it or else you're going to be locked up."

'Crazy' is a term of art; 'Insane' is a term of law. Remember that, and you will save yourself a lot of trouble."

"I am a generous man, by nature, and far more trusting than I should be. Indeed. The real world is risky territory for people with generosity of spirit. Beware."

"There is no such thing as paranoia. Your worst fears can come true at any moment."

"It was the Law of the Sea, they said. Civilization ends at the waterline. Beyond that, we all enter the food chain, and not always right at the top."

"I have long understood that losing always comes with the territory when you wander into the gambling business, just as getting crippled for life is an acceptable risk in the linebacker business. They both are extremely violent sports, and pain is part of the bargain. Buy the ticket, take the ride."

"Freedom is something that dies unless it's used."

"Walk tall, kick ass, learn to speak Arabic, love music and never forget you come from a long line of truth seekers, lovers and warriors."

"I have a theory that the truth is never told during the nine-to-five hours."

Dave Barry
"Guys are simple... women are not simple and they always assume that men must be just as complicated as they are, only way more mysterious. The whole point is guys are not thinking much. They are just what they appear to be. Tragically."

"Not all chemicals are bad. Without chemicals such as hydrogen and oxygen, for example, there would be no way to make water, a vital ingredient in beer."

Dennis Miller
"It's ironic that in our culture everyone's biggest complaint is about not having enough time; yet nothing terrifies us more than the thought of eternity."

"There's nothing wrong with being shallow as long as you're insightful about it."

"Born again?! No, I'm not. Excuse me for getting it right the first time."

Roger Stone
"Always praise 'em before you hit 'em."

"Admit nothing, deny everything, launch counterattack."

"Never do anything till you're ready to do it."

"Look good = feel good."

"Always keep the advantage."

"Never complain, never explain."

Saki
"Few people talk as brilliantly to impress a friend as they do to depress an enemy."

"Words are sometimes given to us to defeat our purposes."

Tenyson
"Into the jaws of Death, Into the mouth of Hell rode the six hundred."

"He makes no friends who never made a foe."

TS Eliot
"Only those who risk going too far can possibly find out how far one can go."

"Home is where one starts from. As we grow older the world becomes stranger, the pattern more complicated of dead and living. Not the intense moment isolated, with no before and after, but a lifetime burning in every moment. And not the lifetime of one man only, but of old stones that cannot be deciphered"

Margaret Thatcher
"The problem with Socialism is that eventually you run out of other people's money."

"If you set out to be liked, you would be prepared to compromise on anything at any time, and you would achieve nothing."

Winston Churchill
"One ought never to turn one's back on a threatened danger and try to run away from it. If you do that, you will

double the danger. But if you meet it promptly and without flinching, you will reduce the danger by half. Never run away from anything. Never!"

"If you are going through hell, keep going."

"You have enemies? Good. That means you've stood up for something, sometime in your life."

"Courage is what it takes to stand up and speak; courage is also what it takes to sit down and listen."

"Kites rise highest against the wind. Not with it."

"Nothing in life is as exhilarating as to be shot at with no result."

"A lie gets halfway around the world before the truth has a chance to get its pants on."

"Man will occasionally stumble over the truth, but most of the time he will pick himself up and continue on."

"I am an optimist. It does not seem too much use being anything else."

"Everyone has his day and some days last longer than others."

"He has all of the virtues I dislike and none of the vices I admire."

"It is a fine thing to be honest, but it is also very important to be right."

"Perhaps it is better to be irresponsible and right, than to be responsible and wrong."

"A fanatic is one who can't change his mind and won't change the subject."

"I have never developed indigestion from eating my words."

"We are masters of the unsaid words, but slaves of those we let slip out."

"I never worry about action, but only inaction."

"It is a mistake to look too far ahead. Only one link of the chain of destiny can be handled at a time."

"Play the game for more than you can afford to lose... only then will you learn the game."

"To build may have to be the slow and laborious task of years. To destroy can be the thoughtless act of a single day."

"I am prepared to meet my Maker. Whether my Maker is prepared for the great ordeal of meeting me is another matter."

Rudyard Kipling:
"Here's to you Fuzzy Wuzzy at your home in the Sudan.
You're a poor benighted heathen, but a first class fighting man."

"For it's Tommy this and Tommy that and chuck him out the brute
But it's savior of his country when the guns begin to shoot."

"When you're wounded and left on Afghanistan's plains
And the women come out to cut up what remains
Just roll to your rifle and blow our your brains
And go to your God like a Soldier."

"Though I've beaten and I've flayed you,
By the living God that made you,
You're a better man than I am, Gunga Din!"

"Down to Gehenna or up to the throne,
He travels fastest who travels alone."

"Ship me somewhere east of Suez,
Where the best is like the worst.
Where there ain't no ten commandments,
And a man can raise a thirst."

"The sin ye do two by two
Ye must pay for one by one."

"Now this is the law of the jungle,
As old and as true as the sky.
And the wolf that shall keep it may prosper,
But the wolf that shall break it must die."

"I keep six honest serving men
They taught me all I knew.
Their names are What and Why and When
And How and Where and Who."

Japanese Proverbs
"The hawk with talent hides its talons"
"A reputation of a thousand years may be earned in the
time of one hour."
"When folly passes by, reason draws back."
"A pig used to dirt turns it's nose up at rice"

"Darkness reigns at the foot of the lighthouse."
"Laughter cannot bring back what anger has driven away."
"Never rely on the glory of the morning, or the smiles of your mother-in-law."
"The nail that sticks its head up is the one that gets hit."
"The tongue is but three inches long, yet it can kill a man six feet high."

Shakespeare, (He's overdone, but these lines from MacBeth are curmudgeonly)
"Men shut their doors against the setting sun"
"We have scotched the snake, not killed it"
"By the pricking of my thumbs, something wicked this way comes"
"When our actions do not, our fears do make us traitors"

Movie or TV quotes (Sometimes we find inspiration in entertainment. It happens)
"It's so refreshing to work with someone who throws a saddle on a gift horse instead of looking it in the mouth."
–House of Cards

"Evil wins when good men choose to do nothing."
-Alcatraz

"All fables are ultimately about the futility of being human."
-Alcatraz

"It is a fool who looks for logic in the chambers of the human heart."
–O Brother Where Art Thou.

"Men come with directions. Find hole (preferably moist), insert, repeat."
-Clerks

"Get ready little lady. Hell's coming to breakfast."
-*The Outlaw Josey Wales*

"Fill your hands you son of a bitch."
-*Rooster Cogburn*

Just because curmudgeons hold little hope for the world doesn't mean we're completely hopeless (even the Chiefs won a Superbowl once for Christsakes), so I'll end this chapter on an upbeat note. This is the one and only poem that I have ever read about hope that I remembered.

I could tell you of heartbreak, hatred blind,
I could tell you of crimes that shame mankind,
Of brutal wrong and deeds malign,
Of rape and murder, son of mine;

But I'll tell instead of brave and fine
When lives of black and white entwine,
And men in brotherhood combine-
This would I tell, you son of mine.
-*Kath Walker*

CURMUDGEON INSULTS

"Comedy always works best when it is mean spirited."
-John Cleese

Curmudgeons love putting people in their place, especially braggarts, the pretentious, and the smug. It's not about being mean. It's about being honest and to an extent it's about establishing dominance. There's definitely a satisfaction in verbally conquering someone who deserves it, but it's more about teaching them a little respect and humility that they might not have otherwise been taught had they opened their mouth around less surly people. So in a way we're doing the recipient of the insult a favor and building his character through embarrassment.

Sometimes it's the best part of being a curmudgeon. We're always seen as irascible and off-putting, so an off-color remark from us isn't a surprise to anyone. Go for it, but keep in mind that insults have to be used with discretion. You can't just go around sticking your fingers in everyone's eye and not expect a backlash. They have to be used sparingly and at the right moment for the maximum impact. And always remember...it's not an insult if it's true.

You're the Easy Button of stupid.

You're the centerpiece in a bouquet of assholes.

You're as necessary as an ice scraper in Miami.

You're thicker than woodpecker lips.

There's a name for you and it rhymes with Jackass.

You're more awkward than the Beastie Boys at Downton Abbey.

You fit in like a bulimic at Thanksgiving.

You're allergic to being correct.

There isn't enough antibiotic in the world to kill the failure cells in your body.

There isn't enough antiseptic in the world to cleanse the failure of being you.

I can fix inexperience but I can't fix stupid so you're hopeless.

Even the Russian judge is giving you high marks for your stupidity and she's a codgy old witch.

You're a Corolla putzing along in the fast lane and I'm a Mustang flashing my lights at you to get the fuck out of my way.

There can be only one. And you're not it.

I'm going to give you a wide berth so your mediocrity doesn't rub off on me.

Good job. You keep aiming at nothing and hitting it.

I expected nothing from you and am so glad to see you didn't disappoint.

I think you were a pirate in an earlier life. You never discovered a toothbrush and you're familiar with the word 'buggery.'

The fact that you mastered bi-pedalism and opposable thumbs are triumphant feats of your evolution.

I can already smell your soul charring over an open pit in hell for this.

You're one of those people fate had the best intentions for but never carried through on.

The only wise things about you are your teeth, and those were pulled out ten years ago.

You're the keystone on the arch of stupid *(stupid can be replaced with anything...moral degradation, ignorance, lazy. Go ahead, give it a try. Fill in the blank for someone you know)*.

You're going to do what? All aboard the bad decision train.

A pound of primer and a suit of bacon wouldn't help you get friends.

You got a new car? Matchbox or Hotwheels?

Isn't it your nap time?

When you hit puberty you can join the conversation.

Keep working on shapes and colors and you'll be a real boy someday.

You're very considerate. Now go practice your war face in front of the mirror until your balls drop.

Do I need to write this in crayon for you?

I'd write this down, but your mommy would have to read cursive to you.

They say parents shouldn't take favorites, but who are we kidding? You were always in last place.

Someone got an idiot-gram in the mail and is doing his best to read it.

You try very hard to bend life until it matches the pages of your favorite books. Too bad all you know is Dr. Seuss.

The quizzes on happy meals are ridiculously easy. Kind of sucks when you bomb it, huh?

I think you should stick with what you know so I dropped a Dora coloring book on your desk.

All alone with your thoughts and no cell phone to tweet them? The horror.

You were going to say something deep and profound but forgot it. The world's loss, eh?

You're going on a date? Will it end in pepper spray again?

Do you have to register online when you move into a new community?

What magic world do you live in where you're not a dick?

There's something about the sound of your voice that triggers my narcolepsy.

You're so talented at being uninteresting you could tell an eyewitness account of 9-11 and make it boring.

This story sounds like a country song.

This is the worst bedtime story ever.

I'll make you a deal. If you sing this in B Flat I'll pay attention.

I don't care about the labor. Just show me the baby.

I'd rather chew on aluminum foil than listen to you one more minute.

I'd swallow a vile of Ebola if it would make you shut the fuck up.

When you speak I can feel my soul sliding out my asshole.

If you don't stop talking I'll reach up your asshole, grab your tongue and flip you inside out like a windsock.

If you have a point, now would be a good time to get to it. My Metamucil is kicking in and there's a real possibility that I'll shit all over your shoes.

They say dogs hear frequencies higher than humans can detect. I really wish your voice was in that range.

Who's suffered scrotal frostbite from doing the things you wouldn't dare and doesn't give a damn what your candy ass thinks? This guy.

No disrespect intended, though you could clearly use some.

Simmer down. I can actually see your panties bunching up.

You're not very quick son, so you better be able to take a lot of punishment.

I think it's great that you want to challenge yourself but when there's no chance of success then what's the point?

Vodka? Why don't you just offer me flavored antiseptic?

I'm about to unleash my inner Assholian on you.

I always had a thing for you. It was disgust, but it was a thing.

If this were the medieval times you'd be a dragon's lunch.

I aspire to festoon my bedchambers with your entrails.

Begone before a house falls on you, witch!

Get thee to a nunnery!

If you fuck up again I'm going to get medieval and mount your head on a pike.

I don't trust anything that bleeds for five days and doesn't die, so no I don't trust you, lady.

You're like a suppository. Itchy and invasive, but ultimately therapeutic because you make me feel better about myself.

CRUDE ALERT!!

You're not just cheap. You're tighter than fish pussy.

You're colder than a nun's cunt at midnight mass.

You could reach into a barrel of pussy and bring out a dick.

You gotta piss with the cock God gave you. And yours is flaccid.

You're wronger than a pedophile in a Santa suit.

You're wronger than a clown with a hardon.

Chuck you Farley. Go back off in your own jack yard.

Your dick is so flat you could spread peanut butter with it.

Your version of a date is a Red Bull, online porn and a sock in the microwave.

Please go back to jerking off to reruns of 'Doctor Quinn Medicine Woman' and leave me the fuck alone!

Whores everywhere will weep the day someone has to take you off life support.

I bet you still feel guilty when your wife sucks your dick. Such a gentleman.

Some women latch onto the title MILF like it's a Medal of Honor because they've earned it. You're not one of them.

Sex with you is like searching for hay in a needle stack. You can do it but it's not worth all the Neosporin I'll have to slather on my digits afterwards.

You're way more promising than prison sex.

I'll stick three fingers in your genitals and bowl you into Pleasureville.

My house is large enough that no one can hear you scream...from pleasure of course.

Do you ever get tired of memorizing safe words?

My sword may be rusty but your sheath smells like a cannery.

You use your mouth for all the wrong reasons.

You have morning breath? My penis can cure that.

I would buy you a drink but your mouth is clearly too small for my penis.

I'd dip that ass in ranch dressing and explore hidden valley.

You stride through life like a painter with no control of your brush and now you have to soak it in turpentine to get all the gunk off.

I'm not an asshole. Gravity is. Look what it did to your boobs.

When I want to earn your respect I'll do a kegstand and fuck your girl because those are the only two things you care about.

CURMUDGEON WORDS AND TERMS

Curmudgeons develop a way to voice their opinion that's graduated from the juvenile vernacular we grew up with. We all have favorite words and need only the slightest opening to use them. If nothing else they're great to throw out just to confuse the crap out of people as long as they're used properly. Nothing is more ridiculous than using a big word when it's not needed.

Take perspicacity for example. It means the quality of having a ready insight into things or shrewdness, but no matter how many times you rehearse it, "I was born with a level of perspicacity you've never seen!" just sounds dumb. If it's not believable then it loses impact, but work one of these words or phrases into a sentence, an insult, a disagreement and you'll emasculate anyone within earshot.

Anathema-A vehement denunciation or curse. One that is loathed, shunned or reviled.
Your young, brash, "in your face" cockiness is anathema to my older, wiser, "I'll rape your soul you when you least expect it" approach.

Apoplectic-Having a predisposition to apoplexy...extremely angry, furious.
When someone bumped into me in the bank line and spilled my bourbon, I became apoplectic and kicked him in the liver.

Apothecary-One that sells drugs or medicines; a pharmacist.
If your apothecary starts all conversations with "Pssst, hey buddy" then you might be an addict.

Arriviste-A person who has recently attained high position or great power but not general acceptance or respect; an upstart.

You won the lottery and moved into an exclusive neighborhood of families who earned their money by working hard for many years and can't figure out why they keep whispering 'arriviste' when you drive a golf cart to the mailbox? Get thee to a dictionary!

Assuage-Make an unpleasant feeling less intense.
A strip bar might assuage the money I lost at the poker table. Someone hail a cab.

Bacchanalian-A drunken festivity.
That was a perfectly bacchanalian party that I'll probably never remember, but will apologize for many times.

Bereft-To leave desolate and alone, especially by death.
I dropped a bottle of bourbon that broke on my driveway. I was bereft of happiness.

Bric-a-brac-Small ornamental objects valued for their antiquity, rarity, uniqueness.
My mother's house is full of bric-a-brac, porcelain dogs, and swizzle sticks.

Bucolic-Of or characteristic of the countryside or its people.
I have never worn a pair of boots in my life because I'm not into the bucolic life.

Cantankerous-Often angry and annoyed. Hard to get along with.
My brother's rancid bunions make him a cantankerous son of a bitch.

Capricious-Prone to changing one's mind frequently.
We turned off Game of Thrones to watch Friends and suddenly you DON'T want to have sex? You capricious wench.

Castigate-To criticize severely, to inflict severe punishment. *Drawing and quartering your body may qualify as castigation.*

Catharsis-A release of emotional tension that refreshes the spirit.
I left my catharsis in San Francisco...and Hawaii...and Thailand. I was in the Navy.

Charlatan-A person who makes elaborate and fraudulent claims of skill or knowledge.
No, I don't believe you can juggle six running chainsaws you Charlatan, but please feel free to prove me wrong. I want to see this.

Comeuppance-A punishment or retribution that one deserves.
Charlatans who prey on the weak deserve a comeuppance of flaming razor piss.

Concomitant-Occurring or existing concurrently.
It's easy to hate businessmen when you worship entertainers. They're concomitant values.

Congruence-Agreement, harmony, conformity.
I have never been in congruence with pimps, pedophiles, or politicians.

Demagogue-A leader who obtains power by means of impassioned appeals to the emotions and prejudices of the populace.
Mark Antony could be called a demagogue for whipping the Romans into a bloodlust while eulogizing Caesar.

Denigrate-To say or do very critical things about or to someone.
Critics denigrate everything because they take pleasure in tearing people down. Curmudgeons denigrate critics because they deserve it.

Dissonance-A harsh, disagreeable combination of sounds.
Every time I watch American Idol I experience dissonance when a Charlatan sings.

Diminutive-Extremely small in nature, tiny.
Good thing I don't have a diminutive penis.

Douchefuckery-The behavioral patterns of an individual who has an over-inflated sense of self worth, compounded by a low level of intelligence who acts ridiculously in front of colleagues. A derivative of Tomfoolery on an infinitely douchey scale.
Westboro Baptist Church is the epitome of douchefuckery, but if you need another example then this book has taught you nothing at this point and maybe you should consult a mirror.

Egalitarian-Affirming, promoting or characterized by belief in equal social, political, economic and civil rights for all people.
I am egalitarian in my disdain for people. They all suck.

Egregiously-Conspicuously bad or offensive (flagrant).
Your very existence is an egregious foul against humanity.

Emasculate-To deprive a man of his male strength.
If we argue I will verbally emasculate you until your mommy comes to piece you back together with PB&J and your favorite blankey.

Endogenous-Growing or produced by growth from deep tissue. Caused by factors inside the organism or system.
My hate for everything and everyone stems from an endogenous belief that the world is flawed beyond saving.

Eviscerate-To take out the internal organs.
Your marriage is so sad it eviscerates your entire life.

Fastidious-Meticulous, paying attention to detail.
My fastidiousness may be annoying, but I never miss an appointment, never waste a minute, and am always right.

Flaccid-Lacking firmness, resilience or muscle tone.
Your argument that Star Wars is better than Star Trek is flaccid.

Gauche-Lacking social polish, tactless.
You wore a hot pink suit to a black tie wedding? That's not artistic. It's gauchey gauche gauche, you douche.

Gestated-To conceive and develop in the mind.
My plan to end that kid's birthday party by filling a piñata with salsa and ketchup gestated for a long time.

Gravitas-A very serious quality or manner.
Too much frugality and gravitas will lead to a heart attack. Live a little, brother.

Gregarious-Seeking and enjoying the company of others; sociable.
Curmudgeons, by nature, are not gregarious unless it's with members of our inner circle of friends.

Guffaw-A loud and boisterous laugh.
Your "Life is like an Oreo" metaphor makes me guffaw.

Hyperbole-A figure of speech in which exaggeration is used for effect.
Whoa there Mister Revere. "The British are Coming" is a little bit of hyperbole don't you think?

Iconoclast-One who attacks or seeks to overthrow popular or traditional ideas and institutions.
Galileo and all those "the earth is round" scientists were iconoclasts who challenged the system. That takes cajones.

Incorrigible-Not able to be corrected or changed.
My TV has one only station. Incorrigible machine.

Indemnity-Having protection from something, insurance.
Earplugs are my indemnity against listening to the stupid shit people say.

Insidious-Causing harm in a way that is gradual or not easily noticed.
A bad marriage is an insidious evil that never ends well.

Innocuous-Having no effect, harmless.
He takes an innocuous position on every matter because he lacks the spine to voice his true opinion.

Intemperate-Not moderate, excessive, especially in the use of alcohol.
It's a history of intemperance that's gotten me here. Thank God for bourbon.

Irascible-Becoming very angry easily. Having a bad temper.
You're out of white chocolate mocha? YOU CAN'T HANDLE THE TRUTH!

Kerfuffle-Disturbance, fuss.
Why there isn't a jam called Redrum keruffles me.

Killjoy-Someone who wants to ruin someone else's fun.
What kind of killjoy objects to Strip Trivial Pursuit?

Languid-Lacking energy or vitality, weak.
The argument that we should get involved in Kraplackistan's Civil War is languid.

Lithe-Readily bent, supple.
People who have a lithe spine are worthless.

Malevolence-Having or showing a desire to cause harm to others.
My words are full of malevolence for a reason. You're an idiot.

Mawkish-Excessively or objectionably sentimental.
Remodeling the basement into a shrine to your first car is a bit mawkish and downright creepy.

Moil-To work with painful effort; to labor, toil or drudge.
Fuck luck. Hard work and good timing are all that matter. Moil on!

Mollify-To appease the anger or anxiety of someone.
If I take the NRA screen saver off my iPad then will that mollify your candy ass?

Narcissist-Excessive love or admiration of oneself.
A narcissist is anathema to a curmudgeon and is frequently the target of our contempt.

Necromancer-A wizard or magician
Your ability to cobble together completely unrelated data and come up with absurd conclusions is astounding. I shall dub thee the necromancer of stupid.

Neophyte-A recent convert to a belief, a beginner or novice.
You may already be a curmudgeon, but after reading this book you will be a neophyte to Curmudgeonism. There's a difference.

Nefarious-Evil or immoral.
Avoid married men who can name their favorite pornstars. They're nefarious people who will just get you into trouble.

Parsimony-Extreme frugality, penny-pincher.
If there is one constant about America it's that we'll race anything, but it ain't cheap. Crew chiefs have to be parsimonious men and make every dollar count.

Pejorative-A disparaging or belittling word or expression.
If you're an idiot then almost everything I say will sound mean spirited or pejorative. Probably some truth to that.

Persnickety-Giving a lot of attention to details that are minor or not important.
I see absolutely no difference between the Chartreuse and Harlequin green swatches, but if you can tell them apart then you're a persnickety one, Misses Grinch.

Petulant-Irritable or surly.
I have found being petulant an effective means of breaking up a conversation that has run its course.

Pithy-Precisely meaningful; forceful and brief.
I'll take a pithy writer with a dash of wit over a witty writer with no soul any day.

Portentous-Of ominous or momentous significance, fateful, foreboding.

As long as there are teenagers with hormones, prom will always be portentous in a young person's life.

Precipitous-Done with great haste without due deliberation.
Tried to be spontaneous and entered a bench press contest despite having never lifted a weight in your life? That's a precipitous decision that you won't make again.

Precocious-Characterized by unusually early development or maturity, especially in mental aptitude.
No I didn't say your baby was precious. I said he's precocious because he can solve algebra problems already. Clearly he didn't get his smarts from you.

Prodigious-Impressively great in size, force or importance; enormous.
"Do you know who I am? I'm a prodigious member of this community!"
"So's my penis. You still have to wait in line."

Pyrrhic-A victory that results in staggering losses or extreme costs to the victor.
After sex I was forced to cuddle. It was a pyrrhic victory.

Rapscallion-One who is playfully mischievous.
I sat my wife down, looked her in the eye and confessed. "I have a mistress. Her name is pizza." She punched me and walked away while I chuckled. I'm such a rapscallion.

Recalcitrant-Marked by stubborn resistance to and defiance of authority.
"You can chew my butt all day, but I must warn you that I have more ass than you have teeth," the recalcitrant man shouted at his boss.

Remuneration-Payment.
God wants to make sure he balances out the world with smart people and idiots, so your existence is clearly remuneration for mine.

Salutary-Effecting or designed to effect an improvement.
Adding an emoticon to the end of your insult is not salutary, bitch. :)

Sardonic-Sarcastic. Cynically mocking.
The chambers of the Curmudgeon's heart pulse with sardonic blood.

Sagacity-The quality of being discerning, sound of judgment, farsighted or wise.
'Score more points' isn't exactly a blinding flash of sagacity, but it's a proven strategy for winning.

Self-Deprecating-Tending to undervalue oneself.
I make fun of myself because I have agoraphobia. It's self-deprecating humor that hides how much I hate public speaking. Booze is adequate self-medication.

Serendipity-A fortunate discovery by accident.
I happened upon a lonely bottle of unopened bourbon in the liquor store. Guess I'll chalk it up to serendipity and take it home.

Skullduggery-To verbally misguide or deceive.
I will rip your eyes out and skullduggery you! Wait...that's not right.

Sourpuss-Someone who gets uptight easily, takes a joke the wrong way.
What does a curmudgeon say during a chess match?
Get off my pawn, kid!

That was funny. Laugh, you sourpuss.

Subterfuge-A deceptive stratagem or device.
Your attempts to water down my bourbon and subterfuge have led to naught.

Surfeit-To feed or supply to excess, to overindulge.
I will continue to surfeit my indulgence and drink bourbon despite your subterfuge.

Surly- churlishly rude or bad-tempered.
I get very surly when you try to subterfuge my bourbon habit.

Surreptitious-Obtained, made or done by deceptive or stealthy means.
Our surreptitious attempt to tunnel under the DMZ and invade South Korea has been discovered. Run!

Sycophant – An ass kissing "yes man."
Surrounding yourself with sycophants screams out, 'I'm an insecure coward who dies a little every time I'm rejected!' Sycophants deserve a slow death. I suggest opera.

Tantamount-Equivalent in seriousness to; virtually the same as.
Drawing and quartering a sycophant is tantamount to a mercy killing since he's such a worthless shit.

Temerity-Foolhardy disregard of danger, reckless.
Most Curmudgeons ridicule the man with too much temerity to know when he's about to get himself into a situation that he can't recover from.

Tempestuous-Full of strong emotions such as anger or excitement.

Revenge sex is a tempestuous offer that I find myself wanting to accept, but the Walking Dead is on. Decisions...

Truculent-Disposed to fight, pugnacious, expressing bitter opposition.
If you bump into me again I will unleash a truculent barrage of displeasure on your unbefuckled ass!

Unbefuckled-Completely made up term that can mean anything from confused to lazy to generally stupid.
Get yourself unbefuckled before a level twelve cleric turns you into a pillar of salt.

Unbesmirched – To detract from the honor or luster of something.
The voices in my head are telling me to trust you, but still...I want my daughter returned to me unbesmirched tonight so I may have to track you with a drone.

Unscrupulous – Lack of moral standards or conscious to guide one's conduct.
The more creative you are the more you have to protect your creativity from the unscrupulous bastards in this world.

Valediction-An act of bidding or farewell, a goodbye speech.
I yelled VIVA DA NANG, slammed a shot, kissed a hot chick, and left like a boss. My valediction is still talked about with reverence at PTA meetings to this day.

Vapid-Lacking liveliness, animation or interest.
I work at an uninteresting and unsatisfying office that leaves me a vapid shell of a man...until I see my paycheck.

Vernacular-The standard native language of a country. An idiom of a certain trade or profession.

You're reading the core of a Curmudgeon's vernacular at this very moment.

Vilify-To revile with abusive or defamatory language.
You can vilify me as an asshole all day, but in the end nothing you say matters, so piss off.

Vociferous-Vehement or clamorous.
I am a vociferous proponent of Curmudgeonism.

Wampus Cat – A creature of folklore, variously described as some kind of fearsome variation of a cougar.
Single men should be respectful of MILFs, wary of Cougars, and carry body armor for the rare Wampus Cat encounter.

Occam's Razor - A rule in science and philosophy stating that entities should not be multiplied needlessly. The simpler of two competing theories is preferable and that an explanation for unknown phenomena should first be attempted in terms of what is already known. Also called the Law of Parsimony.
If you believe in the philosophy of Occam's Razor then you can't believe in government conspiracies because the more complicated a plan and the more people are involved, the less likely it is to be successful or kept secret. A rogue government employee abusing his power is one thing, but a multi-agency cover up is completely unfeasible partly due to the principle of Occam's Razor.

Mea Culpa – An acknowledgment of a personal error or fault.
I will admit fault and declare a mea culpa when you prove me wrong, but I'm betting by your Scooby Doo lunchbox that won't happen.

Pro Bono - For Free.

Women make it seem like a blow job is pro bono, but we all know that we pay for it in the long run.

Quid Pro Quo – This for that.
69

-Persona non grata – A not welcome person.
The person who farts in an airplane is persona non grata.

Ipso Facto - directly translated as by the fact itself, which means that a certain effect is a direct consequence of the action in question, instead of being brought about by a subsequent action such as the verdict of a tribunal.
You slapped my son, so ipso facto I'm going to kick your fucking ass.

Raison d'etre – Reason for existing.
My raison d'etre is raising good kids who contribute to society. What's yours?

Self-Fulfilling Prophecy – A circular pattern of causality.
Idiots produce more idiots. It's a self-fulfilling prophecy.

Non-Sequitur – A statement that does not follow from the logic that produced it.
You killed a unicorn and now there's a blizzard in the Carolinas? That's a non-sequitur.

De Rigeur – Something considered necessary according to fashion, protocol, or etiquette.
Watching a movie solely because it wins an award is de rigeur. If you only watch what everyone else watches then you will only think what everyone else thinks.

CURMUDGEONS IN ACTION

A long ass book about the way you should live your life can get boring and is usually called a Bible. I like to break things up with humor and I'm a curmudgeonly writer, so I get on rants and don't stop until the bleeding is done[9]. Here are some of the stories I've written over the years that have a pronounced surliness to them. Some are just damn funny while others are dominated by a military-theme, so if you're not into that then skip ahead.

Either way this section is designed for you to pick and choose what you want to spend your time on. I hate wasting people's time, so if a story isn't appealing, then move on. But then again, if it's not, re-examine that thing you call a sense of humor.

THE CURMUDGEON
The story that started this whole thing

The older I get the more I hate being around people. Maybe that's not fair. Maybe it's crowds that I hate. But crowds are made up of people; otherwise they'd be called herds or gaggles. They sure aren't prides because they do stupid things, so fuck that. It's people I don't like.

One early morning trip through the Washington DC airport puts me in a bad mood because of the people that surround me. A businessman gets pissed when the TSA agent refuses to let him go straight to the front of the line to get through security. Just past the security area I can't find a place to put my shoes on because a lady has sprawled her entire family out on the benches provided by the airport. A teenager struggles with the English language

---

[9] Red Smith

while she orders a coffee. "Uh...like...me want a mocha. Giggle giggle." As I get money from the ATM, a group of mid-twenties douchebags stands over my shoulder talking loudly on their cell phones. Whether or not they were trying to scam my PIN doesn't matter. Stand somewhere less threatening before I stick a pen through your windpipe, Abercrombie and Fitch. Two teenagers banter with each other while bits of their sausage crossanwich fall out of their mouths to the floor. My mom would have slapped the stupid out of me for that.

I feel like I'm walking through a zoo peering curiously at the bewildering animals on display. Or am I the one truly on display: a fossil of a bygone age? We all made fun of stoggy older folks when we were kids, but they had white hair, napped on your couch, and smelled like menthol. I used to listen to Robert D. Raeford rant about my generation on the radio and laugh at how stereotypically curmudgeon he was. Little did I know the truth he spoke or how wonderful my parents really were until I became one. I'm only forty and barely removed from my physical prime. Just a few years ago I would have dove into a mosh pit without even thinking about it. Now, I get violent when my personal space is violated and need a Red Bull if I plan on staying up past 11, much less have sex for more than six minutes.

I don't expect conformity and believe personal nuances make us unique, but even the most basic social decorum and sense of compassion for others seems to be dead. Waiting on my plane a chick walks past me and drops a napkin, leaving it because she probably thinks, "someone gets paid to pick that up so I'm not going to." Across the gate I see an elderly woman looking for a seat. No one gets up to offer her one so I do.

I wish life were like basic training. I want to leap out of my seat like the drill sergeant from hell and lock everyone's boot heels together so I can put the fear of God into them, which might be the heart of the matter. As a career military man, I expect everyone to have the same sense of discipline and selfless service as me. The reality is that's simply not realistic. Those of us with military experience are truly different from the rest of the world. It either changes us inherently or amplifies the best parts of good people and makes them even better. Soldiers see things in black and white. Do this. Don't do that. 1000 hours means 1000 hours, not 999. There are two types of people-the quick and the dead. Which one are you?

I would entertain the thought of pulling a Georgia O'Keefe and moving out to a desolate part of the country to be a secluded cattle rancher, but I'm afraid of the militant anti-government groups who congregate there. They'd find out I moved in, learn about my military background and try to recruit me to stockpile supplies and await Armageddon. I would refuse, not because they're completely bat shit crazy or because I don't fancy declaring war on the US government, but because I don't look good in their mid-80's field jackets and neo-nazi paraphernalia that they seem to have an abundance of. Besides, I wouldn't be much company to them. Before long I'd bitch about the wide-open prairies, the majestic views, and the unholy clean air.

And that there are no people around.

WHEN THE BODY GOES
Every time I think I'm doing okay, someone is there to remind me I'm not

I'm a recent addition to the quadragenarian club who needs a silly diet like Nutrisystem to drop my love handles. The inevitable spiral into inconsequence that claims us all has officially begun, just as it will for all anyone reading this. Before you morph into an irascible curmudgeon, look for the warning signs:

It started with Curmudgeon Nick when I mentioned that I had recently run five miles in my fastest time ever – 38:30.

"Hmmph," he snorted in that, 'I'll be polite and not say anything, but I really want you to notice that I just said hmmph' way.' I should have ignored him.

"How fast have you run it?" I asked, knowing full well I wasn't going to like the answer.

"Oh...something like 3 minutes," he said. I think he actually said twenty-four minutes, but all I really heard was, "I laugh at you, old man."

Shortly after that I was in Boston training Muay Thai at Mark DellaGrotte's gym. Afterward a skinny welterweight asked if I wanted to grapple. Inside I snickered. I was an above average grappler and had rolled with some very good people, but just two minutes later this feral whelp had handled me like a naughty dominatrix clad in skintight leather with a riding crop. Despite my seventy-pound weight advantage, I had no answers for his skill. He didn't submit me, but the only thing that saved me was brute force. Once again Nick was there to scoff at me from the sidelines.

The final mortal wound to my vapid physical self-confidence came when I entered an intramural swim meet. I swam competitively for years and have continued to swim nearly two miles every week so I entered the competition convinced of my own superiority and sure I would leave the meet with a slew of middle-aged bikini babes asking "who WAS that guy?" in my wake. After all I was in the 35 and up category. How many decent swimmers could there be in this age group?

A lot. I got smoked. Smoked isn't even the right term. I was the meet's dog bone – chewed up and buried in my Speedo's. It was beyond embarrassing. I did nothing to contribute to the team except frighten children in the stands by screaming "FUCK!" when I lost. I have since tossed out my Speedo's because my pathetic performance was surely caused by inferior textile engineering.

I'm under no preconceived notion that I am able to match the physical feats of my youth. After all, it's called getting old for a reason. But since turning 40 it's gotten ridiculous, like God turned off the light switch on my testicles. It's one thing to lose a step, but losing full minutes on a run or a swim that you once dominated is a soul-crushing, bitter pill that undoes all the hard work and therapy I've endured just to believe in myself.

Besides being a lamentation on the natural order of things, there really is a message to this rant. All you young studs out there partying all night and running a five miler the next morning like it's nothing – your days are numbered. The icy cold specter of death might not be loitering at your front porch, but the aches and pains of middle age, which can be considerably worse are coming. The mysterious joint popping, uncontrollable flatulence, and out-of-breath groaning after a mere flight of stairs are salivating to meet you and if you don't think so, there will almost certainly be someone like Nick standing there to prove that you're just fooling yourself.

THE CURMUDGEON UNIVERSE
A conversation about perspective

"Is that Kim Jong Un?" Sean said looking at the TV.

"That dude's in the outer rim," I responded.

"Dare I ask?"

"Outer rim. I'm the sun and he's Pluto."

"So the galaxy revolves around you now?"

"Not everyone's. Just mine." I grabbed a dry erase marker and sauntered to the board. "Let's say this is me." I put a dot on the board. "The people who agree with me and share the same beliefs are Venus and Mercury. Kind of like you right now." I drew two small circles around my dot.

"Awww. You think I'm a god? How sweet."

"Stay with me, Petunia. Next comes Earth and Mars, which represent the people who are like me, but don't always agree. They're good people and I like or respect them, but we don't see eye to eye." I drew more orbits. "The next layer is Jupiter and Saturn who are the people that disagree with me but maybe do it in a respectful way so I tolerate them. I wouldn't hang out with them though, because they're full of gas."

It was an awesome joke. He rolled his eyes, clearly too sober for this deep discussion. "Neptune and Uranus are the people who have a totally skewed point of view and if we ever had a conversation it would probably devolve into 'nuh-uh' and 'you motherfucker!'"

"And Pluto?"

"Total fucking nutjobs you should never interact with."

"Interesting."

"But here's the thing...in their universe, you and I are Pluto. We have right wing beliefs so they think we're the crazy ones. We're the unbending, business-loving conservatives who they think are out in left field, which is fine. Everyone has their own universe and layers of people they surround themselves with. I think that's part of being a curmudgeon; you finally realize that you're never going to change anyone's universe. They have a belief system and are set in it...but so are we."

He paused to think about this mind-blowing truth. "So who's right?"

"The person who has history, hard data, or facts on their side. Capitalists think Communists are on the outer rim. We think they're a whole different bag of crazy, but Commies feel the same about us. So who's right? I'll tell ya who. The one with a hundred years of proof behind them...us. Capitalism has mostly succeeded in every country that has attempted it except the ones who were idiots about it while Communism has failed every time it's been attempted but two and those experiments are getting anorexic." I pointed back to the TV as Kim Jong Un waved to the crowd.

"Pluto."

THE WAR WITHIN
Curmudgeons have a constant war raging within between reality and fantasy

I have a hard time balancing my professional demeanor with my inner street kid now that I'm out of uniform. "I don't want any trouble" is in direct conflict with "I will rip your eyes out and skull fuck you." The attitude I was born with is suddenly in direct competition with the gentleman drilled into me by the Army. At my core I'm fairly violent and not even remotely realistic when it comes to my fighting ability. Even at 42 years of age I feel I can traumatize anyone, anywhere with lightning fast efficiency and devastating power. The truth is I can't and that's the problem with middle-aged men. We think we can do things that we did in our twenties when in fact they are well outside our physical and moral abilities.

The middle aged man needs to realize there's a war being waged in his mind. The struggle between what I *want* to do and what I *can* do is Napoleonic. For example, instinct tells us that mating is good and that we should do it...a lot. In Layman's terms, nature insists that we fuck hot chicks always and often, but reason tells us it's wrong to do so because society has deemed multiple amorous partners as inappropriate or at least taboo enough that giant polygamist families get their own TV show so we can ridicule them. So which one do we listen to…the voice we were born with or the voice of societal norms?

We balance these emotions out by telling ourselves it's a good thing to stay faithful and that nature's call to conquer hot ass is a bad thing, which is completely counter-intuitive to instinct. The strong ignore their urges to get jiggy while the weak succumb to their innate desires and chase tail no matter the consequence. It's a never-ending struggle between instinct and reason that not every man wins. Ockham's Razor tells us the simplest of all solutions is the right one, but in this case the opposite is true. Following a boner is hazardous to a man's soul and even worse…his wallet.

Women don't know or care about this crisis in the least bit. They just want a man they can bend to their will, which is fine as long as they accept that bending them too far may backfire. Push some men across the line and they will snap back like a rubber band, forego reason, give in to instinct and fuck every walking whore he can get his grubby mitts on. Blame God. He made us this way.

THE FIRE WITHIN
It still burns no matter how old you get

My kid's soccer team sucks and when they're getting creamed beyond the point of embarrassment the rage builds up inside. My first reaction is to punch the opposing coach in the face as he runs the score up, but I know that's generally frowned upon and would eternally embarrass my kid, so I refrain.

My second reaction is to take up a sniper position in the trees and shoot the ball…and every other replacement ball that the refs bring in to stop the game. I don't need to explain how bad an idea that is.

My third reaction (and the one I eventually execute) is to shut up and take it. But the game seems to last a fucking eternity and as mature and rational as I am, every second is a moment in hell as my child falls deeper and deeper into self-loathing that I will have to build back up with standard parental phrases like "you did your best" and "it's just a game."

But it's not and we all know it.

Sports are at the core of who we are as Americans. We're competitive as hell and a loss is always bitter whether it's the NFL, an Under-9 Youth Soccer League, or the Retired Fucks Bocce Club of Farmville. Competition is one of the cornerstone building blocks of the red-blooded American and without it, our military would still be a third rate Boy Scout Troop like 1916.

The rage I feel makes me understand how legendary competitors like Michael Jordan, Brett Favre, and Rocky keep retiring from their sport only to don their uniforms one more time to mount a failed comeback. They're wired to compete long after their bodies have lost a step or ten and their sports have passed them by. I'm 43 years old, but completely convinced I can grapple with Tim Kennedy on any given day and hold my own.

The reality? No. I can't.

As disturbing as it might be to get upset over a kids soccer game, it's also comforting to realize that the competitive spirit never goes away. The fire inside me to get down there and show those kids how to beat the living crap out of their competition is a gift that shows me I'm still passionate about something – not losing. If we were comfortable with being second rate, we'd be eating Borscht, singing Das Kapital, and practicing our Goosetep on the weekends instead of watching our kids play soccer.

THE BASKET IS HALF FULL
And it's never the right half

Do you use a basket to transport your laundry? My wife does and she tends to leave the basket sitting on the bed for at least a day when it's clean. So I invariably see it and start to fold the clean clothes. Only I never fold the whole basket. I just fold the things I know I can quickly fold and put away, like my own shirts, jeans, etcetera just to help out. The problem is, my wife will finally get around to folding the rest of the basket and notice that I already did half of it and get mad because to her the basket is half full, not half empty. Instead of being happy that fifty percent of the clothes are done, she gets mad at me for not doing the whole thing. In her mind the half-full basket isn't a gift, it's the sign of some lazy person doing a half-assed job and walking away. In my mind I'm trying to help. In hers I exacerbated the problem and no matter what happens, we have different views on this subject and stand our ground until there's only one solution left: get rid of the basket.

UNIFORMS
Do they define who we are?

Gene Simmons is a narcissistic introvert who oozes old-guy-trying-to-be-young skeeziness while death hungrily watches over his aging frame. But when he donned his stud-riddled body leather, Pimptastic high heels, ghoulish makeup, and battle axe bass to front KISS, he was as close to being a God on earth as Rock and Roll has ever seen. He was a growling, intimidating, fire breathing, groupie-mongering man's man who you simply didn't fuck with for fear of him throwing you through the portal of hell to splash down in the River Styx.

But even Simmons freely admitted to being a completely different person once he removed his makeup and returned to reality. So here's the quandary: does the same thing happen to soldiers, doctors, policemen, or anyone who wears a uniform? Do we act differently when we know we're representing something bigger than ourselves? If so, does that also mean we lose those high standards when we lose the uniform?

I constantly see recently retired Soldiers sporting a gut that eclipses his or her view of their genitalia. They walk around rubbing their bulbous bedsores like Santa Claus and repeat the mantra, "I never used to be this way." In reality they were fat mines waiting for something to trigger them and retirement did the trick. They saw their military career as a race with the 20-year mark being the finish line where pizza intake doubled and buttons popped. Their uniform was the only thing positively influencing their physical behavior and once they lost it they turned obese.

Being healthy is only one piece of the puzzle. Uniforms make us stand up straight and walk tall to represent our chosen profession. Athletes, nurses, firemen, UPS delivery drivers, and even lawyers in suits feel a level of decorum that must be upheld when wearing their uniform. It's a physical reminder of the path we've taken and we don't want to do the uniform injustice. It's a little sad to think that we need it to change our behavior in a positive way, but everyone needs to find something that motivates them to do their best. At least if you give a shit about what you do. If you don't then have another slice of pizza and please don't ever dress up like Gene Simmons.

CUBICLES
In some ways, they're not a bad thing

"I don't want to work in a cubicle," you tell the world as you get ready to retire from the service. "When I retire I'm going to be my own boss. Not gonna work for anyone."

Pump the brakes, kid. Let's think about this.

When you work in a job you hate, in a tiny cubicle, for a giant corporation with asshole supervisors that doesn't give a shit about you, it's easy to turn it off. It's easy to jump out of your seat at 5 o'clock, dust your hands off, go home and forget about it. It's easy not to let it bother you...at all. You can sit at your desk and blankly stare out the window or pretend to do work and still get a paycheck because the profits and losses of the company don't concern you. The corporation could be über profitable or flirting with complete shutdown, but as long as your piggy bank keeps getting stuffed, it doesn't matter.

And if you aren't passionate about the job, you don't leave with it on your mind. You don't get in the car and obsess over how to make it better. You don't look around at every little thing other companies are doing and ask, "how can I do that for my business?"

On the opposite side of the galaxy is the entrepreneur who started a business either because he loves it or he has a syphilis-like burning desire to make tons of money. But here's the drawback – when you do something you love, something that keeps you excited all the time and pervades your soul, you cannot turn it off. Ever. It's always there. Every time you have a good idea or a moment of creativity you ask yourself how can you apply it to your business. Every time you laugh at a commercial, you ask yourself how you can be that funny with your product. Every time you see an ad, a marketing event, or even a protest, you ponder why you are or are not doing those same things or how effective they might be if you did. Owning a business is like having an STD. It never goes away...ever.

The worst part about doing something you love is that you love it more than you should. Everyone around you has to compete with it for your time. Your wife, your kids, your dog, they all want you to snap out of it, stop thinking about the business, and give them some attention. They all want you to put the phone down, step away from the computer, and be there. Really be there too, not blankly staring out the window wondering about the things you think you should be doing. And that's a very difficult thing when you run your own business.

Don't have a family? Entrepreneurialism may be right for you then. But before you make the leap into the unknown, keep in mind that there's something to be said for a job that you just don't give a shit about.

SELFLESS SERVICE
Does the military teach us things civilians don't understand?

"The needs of the many outweigh the needs of the few," Spock said as he died while saving the ship in Star Trek 2. Ole Pointy Ears must have been an Infantryman in a previous life. The difference between the active military attitude and the civilian world's is never more obvious than in the difference between selfish and selfless service. This is by no means a disparaging diatribe on the civilian workforce, so allow me a moment to explain.

When you're in the military, you work until the work is done, no matter how long that is. If your Platoon Leader, Company Commander, or whomever tells you, "we have to get this shit done and nobody's going home until we do," you do it. You bite the bullet, suck it up, and drive on until the mission is complete. You don't say, "my union won't allow it," "am I getting paid any extra?" or "lick balls old man, I quit." When you join the military you forfeit your rights to rebel against the system. Some will tell you the rank structure that we have and harsh penalties for disregarding it ensure discipline within the ranks. Others will say that when there's no rest until the work is done, Soldiers will buckle down and work their asses off until they can go back to the barracks and crash. Both of these explanations assume the Soldier is working because he has to, not because he wants to.

I don't buy that.

I think one of America's greatest strengths is its all-volunteer military force. For the most part, everyone in the military wants to be in uniform. The days of "go to war or go to jail" where military service was seen as a punishment for crime are over. No one forces a citizen to join and we don't have conscription, so the prevailing attitude is one of volunteerism. Once you join you become part of something amazing where you actually give a shit about the warfighter on your left and right. The people who embrace this life want to get the job done and done right. It's called selfless service – recognizing that there's a collective good much greater than the individual need.

Before anyone gets the impression that I'm about to go off on a holier than thou tirade extolling the virtues of military life and deriding civilian life, know this – I'm sure there are civilians with great, selfless attitudes who work their asses off to get the job done and I've met many. However, on the whole, the civilian workforce has an attitude of, "what's in it for me?" which is understandable under the construct of capitalism. That's what they do - be creative, make money, work hard, and make more money.

But in the end it's all about yourself. Sure there are exceptions and it's a generalization, get off my ass. You know what I'm trying to say, but let's look at a simple example - billing hours. Many civilian companies keep detailed track of their employees whereabouts and have them fill out sheets at the end of each pay period detailing how many hours they actually worked. Anything over their normal amount (usually 40 hours per week) is credited to vacation time, sick time, golf, donkey training, animation classes, whatever.

It's this methodical counting of every second and an unbending policy of clearly defined work times that underscores how different our worlds are. There's a set limit to the work and the compensation for it and if it's violated then local law enforcement and unions get involved. In the military, it doesn't matter how many hours you worked. You just work until the work is done. It's all about taking care of your unit rather than taking care of yourself. The measure of success is not how much money you've earned for yourself or your company, but how many lives you've protected through disciplined training and personal sacrifice.

Spock was a damn fine Soldier.

A Sense of Entitlement
Get the fuck over it

'Haha. I wouldn't work for that," Lieutenant Colonel Bighead tells me.

"It's a fair salary," I respond. "Everyone is cutting their budgets now."

"I'm worth more. Find something better," he says hanging up the phone.

This is a real conversation. I was once a recruiter and used to make fun of the Occupy Wall Street kids who squatted on public parks and made unreasonable and oftentimes laughable demands for the world to take care of them like they needed an extra large teet to suckle off of. But now I was getting pretty much the same attitude from a

20-year military veteran with an overblown sense of self-worth.

I'm a huge champion of that oh-so-core capitalist value: a free market economy. And I believe everyone should aspire to capture their market value and then some. If you discovered Einsteinium and you're worth a bazillion kajillion dollars a year, then by God demand it. But here's what most people don't realize...the market dictates a person's value, NOT the individual; and Lieutenant Colonel Bighead doesn't know what I do - that the market frequently turns down sharply and when it does the days of wine and song end.

And now...the rest of the story. In a strange way I'm just as guilty as Bighead. When he copped an attitude the first thing I thought was, "you disrespectful fucko." I didn't like the way this guy talked to me. He's easily four years my junior and in uniform I would have jacked him up until he cried. But that's the exact same narcissistic character flaw that I was pissed about in the first place: that somehow I'm owed something for my service. For a minute I felt like this guy should show some respect for my time in uniform when I realized a blinding truth: no one gives a shit about your service when you take the uniform off...and shouldn't. Your rank, your badges, and your cool beret don't continue into civilian life. It's over and overnight you go from Joe Cool to Joe Bag-O-Donuts when it is. No has to give you respect or recognize your authority. You're rebooted and show up on day one of the new job with a clean slate, so once again...check your attitude at the door.

When the Occupy Wall Street movement was going on everyone (including me) kept telling those kids with an overblown sense of entitlement to 'sack up' and get over it. That's good advice no matter how old you are.

I'M NOT A COUNTRY BOY
You can have your green acres

"I'm guessing you're not much of a golfer," a suit says beside me.

"The only birdie's I shoot don't get up," his newfound friend at the bar responds. I didn't want to look, but the smooth, yet gruff Sam Elliot voice was wet with contempt as he made fun of the city guy. I kinked my head just enough to see a cowboy hat juxtaposed against the bewildered expression of a businessman who was trying to make casual conversation, but instead found himself on the wrong end of an irritated Clint Eastwood. It was an innocuous comment between two people I didn't know in an airport bar while I was half lit on bourbon and a cancelled flight. The curmudgeon in me pleaded with my reasonable side to start an argument, but luckily reason pulled a five-finger death touch and stopped it cold. Still...an inner struggle had begun and I couldn't have stopped it with anything less than beating my head against the bar.

Is there something so thoroughly shameful about being bereft of bucolic instinct that we should feel ashamed for living in major population centers and not knowing if we're driving by alfalfa, cabbage, or carrots when we venture into the countryside? When I drive by a farm and get a whiff of soybeans and cow shit, I think two things: Thank God for Farmers and Thank God I'm not a Farmer. Farming is a backbreaking, dusty crotch, ripped nails, unending suckfest work that makes grown men weep and barely earns enough scratch to keep it going, much less live comfortably from. I respect the people who do it, but it's just not me and I kind of get tired of people like this cowboy at the bar trying to make us concrete jungle dwellers feel like lesser men for not having any country in us.

I like the sounds and smells of Suburbia on a Sunday when I'm sleeping in and not going to church. I got a

Swedish Husqvarna riding mover that I don't even know how to change the oil on. If I were to tell that to this guy, he would most assuredly disapprove, though I'm not sure whether it's for my panty-weight mechanical skills or the fact that I didn't buy American. He would look down on me because I don't know the cud chewing side from the ass end of a cow and most of America thinks it's funny stuff to emulate country folk and emasculate those of us who know the difference between houndstooth and tweed.

I think there's a conspiracy between Cabelas, Ford, and Jeff Foxworthy to make us non-country boys feel like little Susie Homemakers for not being more outdoorsy. Every so often Hollywood gets in on the act with movies like, "The Cowboy Way" that makes city slicking sinners look like haphazard chumps. I got two words for you, Hoss – Brokeback Mountain. Denim and chaps do not provide you with testosterone, much less an infallible air of superiority.

Truth is, I think we need each other, though not in the way you're clearly thinking after that Brokeback Mountain comment. It's like the Yin and the Yang, the balance in The Force, Obiwan Kenobe and Darth Vader. Country folk and city folk balance each other out. One isn't greater than the other. If the great white hunter wants to spend twelve hours in a deer stand waiting for a buck to walk into his line of fire so he can make flavorless jerky and an antler hat rack, let him. And if Armani over there wants to enjoy a frappucino and a scone while bitching about how he had to wait in line to get into a club and then his date with a microwaved sock fell short, well Lamb Chop be damned, this is America and he can do so. So what if he's never run through a cornfield and felt the sweet sting of a sharp stalk leaf against his supple forearms and suffers PTSD from the sight of a tick. His keen eye for a Coach manpurse helps define who the rest of us are not.

Soldiers are even more at risk for having a redneck background than other demographics. The military mindset seems predestined to revert to the hunter-gatherer instinct and many of us go out to the field to train for weeks only to come back in, load the family SUV, and get lost in the Cascade Mountains. Some guys just can't get enough rain and pine straw. Luckily I've beaten that side out of me and convinced myself that climate control is God's way of saying 'stay inside, my son.' My concept of camping now involves a thirty-foot trailer, several propane bottles, and a flat screen TV with satellite hook up.

Sure, I'm no stranger to a torrential downpour, humping through the woods all night, or dragging my footlocker all the way from my Hummer to my GP Medium tent and to be honest, I abhor people who have no survival instinct in them. I've done it and I just don't want to anymore, so I think it's hypocritical to try to make a guy with hair plugs and four-hundred dollar shoes feel inferior because he doesn't sit on a porch swilling homebrew while singing John Denver songs. This is America. Individuality and the pursuit of happiness is what makes us who we are, even if that happiness is being a chain smoking, bulimic gimp that you find morally reprehensible.

My inner rant at the bar was suddenly interrupted when the cowboy gathered himself up to leave and reached to the ground for his bag, revealing a Manchu tattoo on his forearm (Manchu = 9th Infantry Regiment) and turned to go.

"Want to settle up?" the bartender said, holding a receipt that hadn't been paid. I snatched it like Bill Clinton feverishly scrambling after a discarded bra.

"I've got this."

WHEN A LION DIES
A hero passes but Tiger Woods' affair gets more coverage

"How you doing today, Major?" an old guy in jeans and a Polo shirts says to me one afternoon in Afghanistan. I wasn't surprised by the greeting as much as where it happened-in the JOC (Joint Operations Center). My JOC. I was the JOC chief and some old guy had just invaded it like he was Josey Wales and even greeted me politely. Cheers to that, but my only thought was, "who let this guy in here?" Before I could utter as such, a small crest on his shirt that I immediately recognized as the Medal of Honor stopped me in my tracks.

Holy fuck, was about all I could get my mind to think before he shook my hand. "I'm good, Sir. How are you?" I replied, immediately humbled.

His name was Robert Howard and he was about the studliest son of a bitch you'll ever hear about. I call him a son of a bitch with the full reverence of a fellow soldier in complete awe of his accomplishments and because I know that's what he would have wanted. He was the epitome of a grunt, selfless and patriotic, bereft of ego, and made of something few people (myself included) will ever know. He was a last vestige from the days of wooden ships and iron men and it wasn't until his death that I discovered he was the highest decorated soldier since WWII. Besides his Medal of Honor, he had two Distinguished Service Crosses, eight Purple Hearts, five tours of Vietnam, and a tossed salad of bravery that would make the real 300 Spartans at Thermopylae bow in deference. He was Vietnam's answer to Audie Murphy, a man who displayed undaunted courage as frequently as the rest of us catch a cold.

Yet when cancer finally dragged him down like a pack of hyenas swarming an injured lion, he was relegated to the back pages of most newspapers, subjugated to the more important headlines of the day, like which of Tiger Woods' new mistresses came out of the closet.

It's no secret that entertainers are the apple of America's eyes. It's a necessary evil of being a secure, rich, strong country with nary an enemy on the horizon of the two oceans that protect us. We're comfy and lazy and would rather hear about the balloon boy and Simon Cowell's reduced role in the upcoming season of American Idol than pay respects to a man who was killing zips in the jungle while we were learning the phrase, "mommy...poop!"

As much as I'd like to throw contemptuous bags of shit at the walls of the New York Times, it's really our own fault. Americans want to be entertained and we place those who provide our entertainment on a pedestal to be scrutinized on the same level as our elected leaders (which begs the question, why would you want that life?). When asked, the typical American teenager will list Brett Favre, Johnny Depp, and 50 Cent as their heroes instead of true leaders like Dwight D. Eisenhower, Ronald Reagan, or (God forbid) their own fathers.

Act in a movie, hundreds of millions of people watch you get a trophy. Save a life under heavy enemy fire and only the people who were there watch you get a medal. America values entertainment over honor. But you know what? That's just the fucking way it is. Light a little fire of angst in your heart and feed it annually but then get over it.

I want to be angry that we worship actors instead of our brave warriors, but I can't blame people who don't have a care in the world when men like Colonel Robert Howard created it for them. I can only hope they get a healthy dose of perspective (preferably from their responsible parents) and realize America's most precious asset is not Angelina Jolie in her Beverly Hills mansion, but Sergeant Angel Jiminez in his fighting position in Balad.

171

Maybe it's actually a testament to how strong America is that we can put so much importance into something so inane as entertainment. We're so secure in our lifestyle that we can sit around, fat and lazy like ancient Rome, and have the world fan us and feed us grapes while jesters, musicians, and poets make us feel better about ourselves. Nothing can touch us, right?

Brian Williams of NBC News said Robert Howard left behind a grateful nation. Bullshit. Michael Jackson left behind a grateful nation full of weepy basketball fans. Robert Howard left behind a small, yet very appreciative group of people who understood who he was and were proud to meet him, even if it was in a tent in Afghanistan on the eve of his passing. Rest in peace, Sir.

IT ONLY TAKES A MINUTE
Do your goddamn research, Hollywood!

So there I am watching TV when a Bud Light commercial comes on and some jackhole actor is wearing an Army uniform that's more painful to look at than a tabasco enema. I physically wince when I see it. He's wearing four stray stars pinned to his beret, no unit patch, three rows of completely wrong ribbons, long hair, and a pair of binoculars so he looks like some modern day Patton. It's crap and I get irritated, but it's also something that I should expect at this point. Television and movie makers RARELY get our uniforms right and seem to randomly throw anything shiny on a suit to militarize some actor who's never served. It sucks, but it's something we all notice and all live with.

Right now you're thinking, "Dude...chill. It's just a Bud Light commercial." And you're right. On the scale of things that matter, it's pretty low. I should let it go. But I can't because it's so easy to avoid. In our high-speed, superconnected world it takes mere seconds to Google "Army uniform" and get a link to Army Regulation 670-1, which outlines exactly how to wear the uniform. I'm sure it's the same way for the Navy, Marines, and Air Force, but I'm on a rant here and didn't want to take the time to find out...which is exactly the problem.

People (probably some lowly grip) get in a hurry and figure "close enough is good enough." I can't count the number of times I've watched a movie, TV show, commercial, or whatever and seen a uniform that was being worn not just incorrectly, but stupidly. I even saw a Special Forces patch upside down in an old Vietnam flick once. I always chalked this up to ignorance, told myself we were better than that, and let it go. I even ascribed to that urban legend that the uniform was not allowed to be portrayed correctly...that it was required in Hollywood to make military uniforms off just a little bit for national security. Bullshit. There is no such law.

There are uniforms in film that are just a little bit off and then there are the ones that are grossly schmaplicated. To me the really jacked up ones are downright disrespectful. All it takes is five minutes of research and a little respect to get the wear of a military uniform correct. We wear these uniforms with pride and put a lot of care into maintaining them. So when I see some actor portraying anyone from Private Ryan to General MacArthur looking like a dirtbag, it's disrespectful and I'm going to boycott that product.

No more Budweiser for this curmudgeon. Who's next?

ROOTING FOR EVIL
Why do we want the bad guy to win?

"I can't watch this anymore," I say to my wife.

"Why?"

"These are bad dudes. They rape, kill, and foment biker stereotypes. Why should I want them to succeed?"

"Because it's a good show and you want to see what happens next, bonehead."

She's right. It's a very good show, but at the same time they're pressing my moral panic button and I feel ashamed to find myself rooting for the Sons of Anarchy. So much TV content nowadays feature a protagonist that is inherently evil yet we keep watching and even hope that he or she gets away with their nefarious activities. Hollywood does such a good job of building up a character that we want to get behind him even though he does very bad things that we find ethically reprehensible. So who's to blame, us or them?

The Sons of Anarchy, Boardwalk Empire, It's Always Sunny in Philadelphia, The Americans, Shameless, Game of Thrones, Scandal, Dexter, House of Cards, Breaking Bad, Mad Men, and of course The Sopranos all feature main characters who engage in illegal activities like murder, racketeering, drug smuggling, blackmail, torture, payoffs, book cooking, cat juggling, you name it. There's no two ways about it...they are bad people who do bad things.

And yet their characters are presented in a way that you feel like an inept nerd for not being on board with their cause, so you stretch your own moral standing and become sympathetic with the characters. We want the Sons of Anarchy to run guns and get along with the Mayans because we hold out on a flicker of hope that Jacks Teller will see the error of his ways, change the club, and maybe not hide Santa Claus' body in the California redwoods. We want Walter White to succeed in dealing his homebrew meth, Francis Underwood to pass laws for his own good, Dexter to get away with murder, Don Draper to have yet another affair and not get caught by his Sainted wife, and Olivia Pope to solve a crime even if she has to use Presidential power to pervert the law. We get so involved in the characters that we compromise who we are in order to see them win. And that's the scary part. Is our integrity that weak that we can sacrifice it at the altar of entertainment? Are we that easily manipulated by a compelling story? Or are we just so insanely desperate to fix someone?

I think it's a combination of all three. I think we're easily connected to a character and made to feel sympathetic to his cause no matter how wrong it is. I think humans are addicted to the feeling of hope and channel that into a fictional character that we want to change into a better person. And I definitely think we need someone to fix (especially parents like me).

But this is also entertainment. We're Americans and at the end of the day we watch TV to be entertained. That means we need to have a reason to keep watching no matter how bad the hero (or anti-hero) is. If the storyline is good and the characters are interesting then we compromise ourselves in order to see them succeed even if it means rubbing out some unlucky innocent bystander to achieve their goals. The days of a consistently squeaky clean protagonist who does good things and teaches his sons great moral lessons he learned fighting the Great War are over. As sad as that is, I get it.

The modern age has been flooded with so many hard luck, derogatory, and filthy stories from the seedy underside of life that nothing shocks us. Nothing. Leave it to Beaver has no place in this world of thongs, blowjobs, crack, implants, and chicks in thongs giving blowjobs to get crack and implants while dropping more F-bombs than the Memphis Belle. June Cleaver is too sterile and generic. We need hard hitting cop dramas, life-or-death ER rooms, a Southwest drug war, high stakes 1950's infidelity, medieval incest and torture, and a scorned housewife who slashes off a penis in the middle of the night just to arouse our interest. In this day of 1000 channels, if it doesn't make my jaw drop, then why watch it? I have the power to watch anything at anytime, which raises the ante on Hollywood. So the viewer has a powerful bloodlust like never before and who's really to blame for it?

Hollywood is a profit motivated market and one of the most cutthroat of all. With every movie made, millions of dollars are at stake and the competition to break into the industry is incredibly tight. Take it from a guy who has tried for years to get his screenplays noticed by anyone…this field is tighter than a nun's cunt at midnight mass. So can you really blame Hollywood for using their talents to make money even if it means manipulating your feelings and making you question who you are? Or do you, the viewer, who's so easily swayed away from your own moral base really hold the rose of blame? Are they just giving us what we want and if so, why do we want it so much?

Cooking meth and selling it on the street is as vile and anti-social as it gets, so we're revolted by this kind of activity in real life no matter who's doing it. Yet as you watch Breaking Bad you see Walter White's motivations and his constant struggle to overcome the obstacles created by law abiding citizens placed before him and those who are even worse than him so you cheer him on. Cook baby cook! Sell it on the streets Jessie! Kill those rival drug lords because they deserve it and you don't!!

Watching that show and any like it where the protagonist is morally and ethically fucked creates a conflict inside us. Do I want to fix Walter White and Jacks Teller or am I really the one who's broken here? Maybe that's why we keep watching. It's not about them so much as it is about us. In that case I'm glad I stopped watching.

STAIRWELLS
My favorite place to find relief

We all have microorganisms in our bowels that digest the stuff we eat and then let off waste in the form of gas that builds in your lower intestines until you feel pressure to release it. It's usually a mixture of methane, nitrogen, oxygen, and CO_2, depending on what you ate 8 hours ago. Farting is a biological fact that happens to all of us and is the body's way of saying, "shit is about to happen." Yet, despite several Wikipedia pages on flatulence, it's socially unacceptable to do it, admit it, or even talk about it. Some of you are cringing just reading this, and some of you at this very moment feel the pressure building up and need to find an outlet for it.

I work in a cubicle farm where the "walls" are merely four foot dividers that even Gary Coleman could look over. If I were to let my sphincter vibrate and expel the gasses inside it, I'd quickly become "that flatulent guy" and have a stigma forever. Getting over the death of disco was too traumatic to endure another episode like that again. Sometimes it's fun to gross out a car of wasted college kids while following the paper boy at 0500 and picking up all the papers he throws out, but that's a rare acceptable scenario that justifies ass gas. To relieve my pressure at work I choose stairwells. There are three in my building that I am particularly fond of.

The first one is tight and runs from the top to the bottom of the building, which increases the risk factor of playing a one-man round of "pull my finger." Its carpeting muffles sound well, but there are so many turns and floors, I can never tell if anyone is in there with me. I could step on a duck and then turn the corner to find my boss staring me in the face. Not being terribly witty on my feet, I would probably blurt out "whoever smelt it dealt it!" Forget any ideas of promotion.

The second stairwell is halfway between the cafeteria and my cubicle, so I have time to walk and let the jumpers shuffle their way toward the door. It's a big, open space that only has one switchback so I can see everyone in the area. It branches off into the designated smoking area so it reeks of cigarettes and covers most air biscuit odors. But the big space is empty, which only tempts me to squeeze out the cloth ripper just so I can hear it echo. I always fear letting a loud one go will happen just as someone is returning from their smoke break, but this hasn't stopped me from tempting fate.

The last stairwell is one of those grandiose, double stairways that you see in European palaces, only this one leads down into a cafeteria and deposits you in the middle of many tables. The sounds of patrons chewing and talking covers everything, so I can get away with bubbling up the ghost, but it's a double-edged sword. The eau de ass is difficult to mask because my farts don't just float away harmlessly. Like grenadine in orange juice they tend sink to lower atmospheric levels, so as I'm walking down a replica of the Titanic staircase, the air that was recently in my colon has already beaten me to the dining area. Ruffling the cheeks here after a night of chili and beers is unwise.

When you think about it, farts are a design flaw. We should have a chimney on the top of our heads and they should be the center of social attention when someone belches one out. "I feel the same way myself" should be just as common as Gesundheit.

THE CROP DUSTER
Annoying co-workers provide us with great opportunity to illustrate the concept of supply and demand. They demand humility so you supply the methane.

To: Office All
From: Betsy Flanders
Whoever continually passes gas in my row of cubicles, please stop. It's not only impolite, but makes us less efficient since we have to vacate the area for a short period of time while your noxious fumes are slowly evacuated through the building's ventilation system. It's rude and distasteful, so please don't do it anymore.
-Betsy
—

To: Betsy Flanders
From: Jim Connors
Betsy,
I'm not sure who keeps doing it, but they need to be blanket partied. That's how we'd handle it back in the Army. The last thing I want to smell is the air that was recently inside someone's colon unless they ate potpourri for breakfast and washed it down with a vanilla bean frappuccino before crop dusting our row. That would smell pretty sweet, even after intestinal processing, don't you think?
-Jim
—

To: Jim Connors
From: Betsy Flanders
Jim,
I'm not sure that eating air freshener would help with this problem, nor would drinking coffee since this person probably already does (don't we all? LOL). I also don't think blanket partying is the right answer, though I admit I'm not

really sure what it means. But it sounds scary. This person just needs to stop.

-Betsy

—

To: Betsy Flanders
From: Jim Connors
Betsy,
I don't think I just heard you laugh out loud since you're only three cubes away from me. Working in such close proximity to each other is like being on an airplane-it's very easy to get into everyone else's business (and easy to smell each other's business too) LOL (did you hear me actually laugh out loud just now?).
Blanket parties were the vigilante justice that kept the Midwest together in the formative days of this country, but if you don't like that method, how about getting torches, pitchforks, and other farming tools and running the "eau de toilet offender" out of the office like Frankenstein? Would that be politically correct? Or should we just make a false claim of sexual harassment and get them fired the way Peter was run out of here?

-Jim

—

To: Jim Connors
From: Betsy Flanders
Jim,
I don't think you used "eau de toilet" correctly. That's French for perfume. And what did you mean by that crack about Peter? You're being rude, Jim. I just want the smell of man butt around my workplace to cease.
There it is again! Whoever keeps doing it just did it again! I didn't hear anything or see anyone walk by because I was typing this. Did you see anyone?

-Betsy

—

To: Betsy Flanders

From: Jim Connors
Betsy,
I didn't see anything just now except a polar bear pass by
the northern window. This crop duster must be a ninja, so
I'll be sure to keep a suspicious eye out for anyone of
Japanese descent. What makes you so sure it's a man by
the way? That sounds sexist. Can't it be woman butt? Don't
females bubble the ghost occasionally? I know it's not
attractive to think about, but women take craps too, right?
Unless you're like a sloth and excrete waste through your
skin as a defense mechanism to keep predators away (like
Peter). In that case, you would be the perpetrator here,
right?
-Jim
–

To: Jim Connors
From: Betsy Flanders
Jim,
This has gone too far. You're being mean now. I'm easily
emotionally traumatized. We have a problem that needs a
solution. No one should have to put up with farters in the
workplace. Even if this person just went to the stairwell to
relieve pressure, that would be better than walking down
our row and doing it.
-Betsy
–

To: Betsy Flanders
From: Jim Connors
Betsy,
I really don't want to hurt you (isn't that an 80's song?) and
I'm sorry if I'm causing you pain. I sometimes forget how
easily civilians are rattled, kind of like this reporter I knew in
Afghanistan before he got injured (his name was Peter,
ironically). I just want to help find the office flagellator
before you're permanently damaged.

It could be the person who's releasing these air biscuits has Chrones disease and is unable to regulate their bowel movements and is actually pooping his or her adult diaper at their desk. In that case it would be inconsiderate of us to label this person as a farter when in fact they're sitting in a warm pile of last night's corn and kielbasa, too ashamed to get up and go clean themselves. In that case they'd be the company pooper. What a nickname!

-Jim

—

To: Jim Connors
From: Betsy Flanders
Jim,
It doesn't matter what we label him and the thought of someone sitting in their own...#2...is just sickening. Whether it's solid, liquid, or gas, I don't enjoy the odor this person is putting out and we don't have to stand for it. If you have a solution to the issue, please say so. Otherwise, just let me get back to work.

-Betsy

—

To: Betsy Flanders
From: Jim Connors
Betsy,
Didn't we all sit in our own poop as toddlers? Didn't you make stinkies? And if by "work" you mean getting back to your chatting on Facebook, then go ahead. I'm going to take action. I'm going to set a trap for this person. You know that chemical they put in pools that makes pee turn green? I'm going to find a chemical that does the same thing to the air. When this person walks by stinking up the place, the air around him will turn a fluorescent green. Then I'll throw a fishing net on him (or one of those man-trapper nets like in Planet of the Apes) and then you nail him with a baseball bat until he stops moving.

-Jim

–

To: Jim Connors
From: Betsy Flanders
Jim,
Your propensity for violence is disturbing. First the blanket party comment then advocating we beat a man (okay...or a woman) until they stop moving? Are you sure you're recovered from your time in combat? I'm not sure I'm comfortable with sitting in your row anymore.
-Betsy

–

To: Betsy Flanders
From: Jim Connors
Betsy,
Recovered? Probably not. I once went to Dunkin Donuts and ordered a Boston Cream Pie doughnut, but instead I got a cream-filled chocolate one. It did terrible things to my insides. I tried to sit quietly in the store and enjoy it anyway, but the clerks kept going off in Arabic, saying something about the smell (of the doughnuts I assume) that was keeping the customers away. My friend (the one I told you about from Afghanistan) told them it was their own nasty body odor that made the place so foul, but they persisted. So I flipped out and beat them up pretty badly with a one-gallon milk carton (those things are heavy, huh?). It was really messy.
-Jim

--

To: Office All
From: Betsy Flanders
I will be out of the office indefinitely.
-Betsy

I DRINK FOR A REASON
Most of us drink, but do we all know why?

The most often noted reasons for imbibing in alcohol are to feel good, forget painful moments, or take the edge off a long day of "What the fuck are you doing ass hat?" But we're all individuals. We all have our reasons for hitting the bottle, taking a nip, and living life by the drop. Time to confront those demons once and for all.

I drink because there are things in this life that I will never have no matter how many times I steal them.

I drink because "if you can dream it, you can achieve it" is bullshit unless you have a twenty-inch schlong, an artistic eye for camera angles, and a group of very gullible hotties.

I drink to overcome the guilt of not deploying as many times as all my buddies.

I drink because I lost one of them and had to find out through a newspaper.

I drink because I live in a country where Green Bay, Wisconsin has two Superbowl rings and Los Angeles doesn't even have a team.

I drink because I still don't understand what the fuck extra virgin olive oil is and why it turns me on.

I drink because I have a daughter who is not a horse-faced troll with protruding teeth that could eat apples through a picket fence. Life would be easier if she was.

I drink because there are, and always will be, ignorant Americans who simply cannot fathom why those of us in uniform do what we do.

I drink because there are still poor, unfortunate souls who know neither victory nor defeat.

I drink because I am a fool who hopes logic dwells in the chambers of Congress.

I drink because I am confused and I am confused when I drink. Such is the sweet circle of distilled spirits.

I drink because I can't remember what I just said.
I drink because I can't remember what I just said.
I drink not to silence the voices in my head, but to
understand them better.
I drink because society deems it unacceptable to festoon
my bedchambers with the entrails of my enemies.
I drink because those who have made the ultimate sacrifice
can't.

LET'S GET DRUNK
Is there any better advice for any situation...ever?

Don't feel like going to class? Let's get drunk and blow it off.
You're a lazy, illiterate shit and text a lot? LGD.
Your son lost a basketball game? Let's get drunk (assuming
you weren't already drinking at the game).
You got drunk and made an asshole out of yourself at a kids
basketball game? Let's get drunker.
The Red Hot Chili Peppers are coming to town? Let's get
drunk under the bridge.
Lost a buddy in combat? Let's get drunk for your brothers in
arms.
Successfully crossed the border with illegal paraphernalia?
Let's get drunk after you pull the bong out of your bung.
Flying across country in the middle seat? Let's get drunk.
And drunker. And even drunker. Flying sucks.
A liberal was elected in your district? Let's get drunk and
stay that way for four years.
You had a threesome and realized one was actually a dude.
Let's get drunk...and never speak of it again.
Went bankrupt on a ponzi scheme and have to move into a
trailer? Let's get drunk on PBR.
Had a bad day at the office and the flask you got as a
Christmas gift is still full of whiskey in the top drawer? Let's

get drunk and send inappropriate emails to the boss. That's always a good idea.

The hottie in your office blew you off because you got drunk and couldn't think of a pickup line? Let's get drunker.

You went home and loaded up all your guns to go shoot up the office? Let's cool down and then get drunk until you pass out.

Someone called the cops, they came to your house, and they found the arsenal you were going to use to shoot up the office? You're screwed. Better get drunk while you can.

THE LIFEGUARD OF SHAME
Courage conquers

People who have a job that involves the health and welfare of other people but don't take it seriously have reserved seats in the first class cabin of the plane to hell.

I'm swimming laps one day when I notice the lifeguard is gossiping with a friend and has her back to the pool. Were this a momentary respite from paying attention to all the swimmers I might not have cared, but fifteen minutes into my workout and these chicks have their faces mashed together like they're making out. It only takes a second for a tired swimmer to go under and less than thirty for them to drown permanently, so a lifeguard's attention should never be diverted especially for trivial girly gossipy shit. If they're solving world hunger then I could understand but there weren't enough brain cells between these two to play Chutes and Ladders.

I don't care about how people look at me, but the last thing I wanted was to bitch about these gals and have it affect my kids. The lifeguard and her bosom buddy were high schoolers with siblings in my son's class. I didn't want to be that parent that embarrassed him unintentionally because when I embarrass him I want it to be on my terms and totally on purpose.

But this was wrong and people like her are the moral panic buttons of society: they're in a position of responsibility who have a direct impact on whether or not someone lives but don't care. It was completely irresponsible and no amount of popularity is worth letting such an infraction go unnoticed.

"Excuse me," I said taking a break in between intervals. "I'm swimming my ass off here and am getting fatigued. I'd hate to think if I go under you won't notice it because you're not paying attention."

"Oh we're just talking. I know what's going on."

"Really? Well then tell me..." I'd taken a lap to think about my response in this situation. "without looking...is the lady in lane one using a pull buoy or not?"

She turned and looked and looked and looked some more. "There's no one in lane one."

"Yes, but you didn't know that until just now, did you?"

She rolled her eyes and her friend smirked. She was at a decision point. She could do the right thing and stop talking to her friend or tell me to fuck off and keep doing it. She chose the right path and went to her lifeguard chair with a new enemy in her life while her friend shot me a look of death and swam away. Doing the right thing sometimes means being a dick or forcing yourself to overcome an aversion to confrontation so others learn a valuable lesson. Viva la Curmudgeon!

FINDING BIGFOOT
The story of a curmudgeon chasing an elusive Sasquatch
with clever metaphors about old-age and new discoveries
that ruins everything he thought he knew about life.

Hangovers are nothing new and in fact I'm alarmed sometimes at how comfortable I've become with the dull headache and stiffened joints of overindulgence. They're my friends, however inconvenient and at least the pain affords me the comfort of knowing that I'm still human and still in control of something. I can cause the pain or I can medicate the pain away.

"What's wrong with me?"

"You really need my dumb ass to explain it?" Randy says.

"Isn't there supposed to be wisdom in the mouths of babes and backwoods rednecks? I stand in Starbucks and stare at the back wall like a zombie. I try to disappear hoping no one will try to talk to me. Nothing makes me say, 'I can't wait to do this' anymore."

"Then you need to do this! Haha!" he points at his phallic shaped parabolic microphone. He's crazy. And I'm not talking unfit-to-stand-trial crazy, but does-the-stupidest-shit-for-no-reason crazy. Like he was born without the neurons that tell a body it's in danger. He's either insanely brave or bravely stupid. After twenty-two years, I still can't tell which.

"How the fuck did you convince them suits to git you up here, anyway?"

"Research. We need to know how some of our new detection devices work in the wilderness."

"So you got my tax dollars to pay for your vacation?"

"I wouldn't call it a vacation. South Padre Island was a vacation. Lake of the Ozarks was a vacation."

"When you went after that Amazon basketball player?"

"You're destined to burn in hell you know that?"

He laughs; the man sign that he'd won this verbal sparing. And he did. "This is research. I'm working." It's a feeble attempt to scrounge up some dignity.

"I don't see you working."

"I don't see you doing...whatever the hell you do anymore. What do you do?" *And how did we ever become friends again?*

"I'm a firefighter. We both run towards the trouble, not away from it."

And there it is. As crazy as he is we're two peas in a pod especially since we both have a sense of urgency to help others though he just calls it his "Git R Dun" side. Say what you will about Bigfoot and the crazies that chase them, but I find it easier to believe in the existence of an elusive giant ape than I can a productive Congress, which is proven to exist. Sasquatch is just an animal and zoologists find animals in nature that we didn't know existed all the time. At one time we were absolutely sure nothing could live on the bottom of the ocean because of the intense pressure and freezing temperatures, but in fact it's teeming with life. So why is it so hard to believe that a large North American ape lives out in the farthest reaches of woods where few humans ever venture?

"So let me tell you what you're up against," Randy says on the marathon drive to his campsite. "They're territorial. They throw heavy objects to scare people away. They growl. Their stride is different. They have shorter legs, but a longer stride because they're taller. Seem to glide instead of jerky gallop like us. Their call sounds more like the death scream of a jizzing teenager than an animal. They pace when watching people and like to knock on wood to scare people away. They eat plants..."

"Not only plants. I think they're omnivores," Andy the sidekick interrupts. "They kill a deer on occasion. I've found deer with one leg removed only. No way a hunter'd do that. Bears don't do that."

Randy nods. "They're really versatile with their diet. They don't have to worry about killing prey if they can't find any. They're the top of the food chain already."

"No...we're at the top of the food chain," I interupt. "Not because of our physical abilities, but because we've learned to gain an advantage through technology." And by technology I mean a gun, which I run my fingers across to ensure it's still in my bag. Like myself, Randy enjoys the feel and firepower of a nine millimeter Beretta and loaned me one because I'm used to carrying in an unfamiliar situation and don't feel like changing now. Some would say this is irresponsible especially in a National Park, but in the hands of a skilled operator it adds security to the situation, not danger. I don't have any issue with those who advocate gun control. I know exactly how to control mine.

"They're not harmful to humans," Randy says throwing logs into a pit some hours later. "I even think they're more human than ape really. I mean if there's a fifty-yard line where you cross over from one to the other, they've done it. They care for their young and teach them like we would. I've seen it. They avoid hunters for a reason and sleep in the open so they don't have to make structures cause it'd draw attention."

I'm not sure I buy this last part, or at least I don't want to. That would indicate an intelligence level that I'm not prepared to accept among long lost primates. "So you consider yourself a serious researcher? A scientist?"

"What else do I look like, a fucking clown? I don't need no goddamn degrees to know there's something out there we don't understand and need to."

He stares me in the eye, daring me to challenge his position. Sure he's not a true researcher in the traditional sense of the word, but he's also doing exactly what traditional scientists do-trying to answer an unanswered question about nature and life in general and using the sacrosanct scientific method to do so, whether he knows it or not. You can't fault a guy for that no matter what his beliefs are. He looks around, knowing he'd nearly lost his temper. He's probably been through this a thousand times from people who told him he's crazy and I just made it a thousand and one.

"Sorry man, I didn't mean to..."

"You seen any casts?"

"Uh...just the ones on my own legs."

"Oh yeah. I remember that," he laughs and moves to the back of his truck.

"This is pretty cool," Andy says tapping my leg. He returns with a hard briefcase and pops it open to reveal a cast of a Sasquatch footprint, the sheer size of which gets my undivided attention. It's a Frankenstein foot with oranges for toes.

"Jesus wept! Is this real?"

"I got it near here."

"How near?" I finger my sidearm once again.

"Near enough," he laughs. "Sometimes the prints double back on themselves cause they're smart."

Again I'm not cool with thinking these things think like us. There are no documented deaths attributed to Sasquatch and yet I feel a direct physical threat to my well-being out here especially with nightfall's suffocating apprehension steadily exerting its inevitable influence over daylight. I shudder and hope they don't notice. "Why do you do this?" I can't stop myself.

Randy sighs and looks into the dark recesses of his mind like a troop recalling a bad firefight. "I had a moment," he says placing the cast on the ground and removing his cap like an old man wanting to tell his grandson about Normandy. "Chickasaw park in Oklahoma.

A bunch of friends told me about Bigfoot so I decided to see for myself...I was young, dumb, you know the deal. On some sorta quest I guess."

Somewhere a pot was calling a kettle black. Randy is two years older than me so he's had his midlife crisis. Mine was prime time.

"It was cold. The off season. No one was there, so I set some bait. Had a gun with me. It was illegal as all get out in a National Park, but I didn't know what I was up against, so I wasn't taking any chances. Still don't. I taped up my truck with blankets so nothing could see inside and I'm sitting there waiting for something to happen. Few hours later I hear these footsteps and I was thinking 'no way!' I mean there was no way on my first time out there, right? But I could hear something rooting through the trashcans behind the truck. It was going from one to another digging in all of 'em and dragging a stick through camp, tapping lantern posts."

"It?"

"Something big."

"But you couldn't see. You had blankets on the windows."

"Well hold on big'un. Let me finish. Yeah, I was like Hellen Keller at an orgy, but I put it all together. You know how they say when you lose one sense the others get better? I could hear everything and I wasn't totally blind. I could see out the mirrors behind the truck right? So I see it move forward and stop and that's when I realize that if I can see it, it can see me."

Makes sense. Like tracer rounds, mirrors work both ways.

"So it stops all of a sudden and I think it's looking at me in the mirror of the truck. And not just once. It looks in my mirror again and again and I'm frozen stiff because it damn sure ain't no person."

This is the worst bedtime story ever.

"I'm thinking it must have smelled me."

"Like I can smell you now," Andy laughs, but we ignore him though it was a nice break cause I'm freaked the fuck out.

"So it takes the stick and hits the truck with it. WHACK! Loud as hell. Next thing I know a second one joins the first one."

"A second one?"

"The knocks are an invitation," Andy interrupts. This I understand because it sounds exactly like a scout who goes into an objective first and when he thinks it's clear he gives a pre-determined signal to the rest of the unit. It's recon 101, but more importantly it shows intelligence which I've noted before has me intrigued. The more I hear the more I think we're not dealing with a dumb ass animal.

"So another one joins it from across the creek and I'm full on scared when I see two of them step out of the woods. Their arms were swinging like gorilla movement. Next thing I know the little one disappears and I think they're leaving right?" He shook his head. "The big one grabs the rack of my truck and looks over the cab to see the tent I set up!"

"It was in your truck?"

"In the bed of my damn truck!"

"What were you thinking?"

"Please go away," he laughs. "The whole truck squatted down like I had a load of coal in it. This thing rummaged through the bed for a few seconds and finally it runs off with my propane tanks. I could hear them clinking together as he went away."

"What did you do?"

"Didn't move until the sun rose, brother!" We all chuckle, but then Randy stares into the fire like he's in Chickasaw again. "It's a helluva moment. Facing your own death like that. Changes you."

Not to be outdone Andy goes into his virgin Sasquatch story, but I'm not listening. Before I hoped and prayed my Bigfoot cherry would pop this evening and went through the best and worst case scenarios for it to happen while at the same time telling myself I was an idiot to actually want a terrifying incident to befall me. But I wanted to know more. I needed closure or at least the satisfaction that some mysteries aren't mysteries at all. The world really is just as plain as it seems and there are no mystical, elusive things out there. It's either a plain old ape or it's not real, right?

We sat another hour waiting for the absolute creepiest conditions to set in and they sure as hell did. The night was damp and the air of uncertainty hung over us. I was Jack Ryan telling himself to write a memo next time.

Randy and Andy prepped their gear and I could see these lovable good ole boys hosting their own backwoods TV show even though my TV is so saturated with them that I feel like I've seen the world, but not in a good way. I'm really tired of saying, "I gotta go there someday" knowing that I never will. I want to see the world. I want to sit on a bamboo deck in the Daintree Forrest. I want to ride a gondola through the Bay of Kotor and drink Glenfidditch on the shores of Loch Lomond. The truth of the matter is it will never happen and even worse I'll never be the one discovering these places because they're all on the beaten path now. So I'm going to die wanting more than I could ever have thanks to the damn Travel Channel. I could have lived an ignorant life never knowing those places exist, but now that I do I will go gently into that good night unfulfilled.

Finally we squashed the fire and go hunting...or researching I guess. We walk for hours with cameras and microphones at the ready, our weapons of choice against this mysterious adversary. Their goal was clear. They seek that home run piece of evidence that not only establishes the existence of Bigfoot and turns zoology and cryptozoology on its head, but also places them on a pedestal of discovery with Magellan and Armstrong. Laugh all you want about comparing them to those pioneers, but in their minds (and increasingly in mine) their dedication to discovery is no different at all.

No matter how badly I want or don't want something to happen it just doesn't. We must have trudged five or six miles and didn't see or hear a single thing out of the ordinary. I guess I should have expected it. If Sasquatch sightings were so easy that a Bigfoot virgin like me would have one on his first try then what would the mystery be? Everyone would see one like they were going to the zoo on a Sunday afternoon. Maybe we should just build a duck blind and charge admission with a sign inside: "Not responsible for extreme boredom or being shredded to bits. Risk incurred by patrons."

The next morning I'm sore. Knees, ankles, and back are feeling the aftereffects of the hike. I'd considered walking the Appalachian Trail until this moment. After being out in the woods with these guys...fuck that. And we only went a few miles with small packs.

"How ya'll doin' today?" an unfamiliar voice asks.

"We're good Bill. You?" Randy answers. I peak my head out of my tent and see a Park Ranger truck parked next to ours. How did I not hear him pull up?

"Get any action last night?"

Randy shrugs. "A few coyotes on thermal. Maybe a howl, but it was pretty far away." Randy fires up the propane stove to whip up some eggs and bacon. I stand, stretch, and nod at the Ranger. He returns the acknowledgment, but something was off. Randy is an honest man who wears his heart on his sleeve, but he won't make eye contact with the Ranger and only makes idle chit chat. If this was a first date Bill would do well to end it quickly cause he clearly isn't getting any. It's ten awkward minutes before he leaves.

"What's that all about?" I ask.

"Nothing."

"Bullshit."

"They know," Andy says.

Randy nods his head and takes a bite of bacon. "Think about it. If we prove they exist how many people would come to a National Park?"

"A ton!"

"Zero. Families are their demographic and main source of income. The Park Service is always strapped for cash, so if we find something that scares away all their customers..."

"So the Park Rangers are keeping tabs on you to see what you know like some sort of Commie Secret Police? That doesn't sound like a conspiracy theory to you?"

"If we prove they exist the only people who would ever come here would be rednecks and researchers."

"Like you guys?"

"Exactly. You want us taking over a National Park?"

"The loggers'd be pissed too," Andy offers. "If a giant tract of land suddenly became a sanctuary for some endangered species they'd lose all their income."

"Sounds like you've got a dilemma then. If you know your discovery will cause economic turmoil then why do it? Why not just let them be if they're really out there?"

Silence. I struck a nerve. Somewhere in the depths of their souls these guys were struggling between individual glory and the common good. Finding Bigfoot again was their passion, but then what? Keep it to themselves or bring one of the most hotly debated shadow creatures into the light? Would mankind even want to know about this or remain blissfully unaware? Even if they got perfect evidence would anyone want to believe it? It was the stiffest moment of the trip. Or so I thought.

"Now what?" I ask pulling my sweatshirt on.

"Try again."

I expected as much. That day may have been the most boring of my life. It was what I envision Survivor being like, but less hungry. Those poor schleps eat only the coconuts they find on the ground while we had anything and everything we wanted and in fact I was a little surprised at how much unnecessary grilling Randy and Andy did. I don't think the fire went out all day and there was nary a moment when the scent of seared meats didn't fill my nostrils.

Dusk nears and I expect to gear up and go hiking again, but neither of my guides seem interested in doing much more than barbecuing yet another hunk of cow. Randy sets his camera up on a tripod and aims it toward a nearby ridge to dial in his settings before realizing that seared meat left in the hands of Andy would result in medium-well steaks versus the medium-rare that he preferred.

"Give me that," he demands taking the tongs. "We'll go a little later. After those boys head out."

"What boys? The ones down the way there?" I ask turning due west and staring into the setting sun like an idiot. Most of the day another party had an encampment that was barely visible through the trees in the same direction Ranger Bill had driven off. I noticed at least one teenage boy and an older man and assumed it was a vacationing family. Maybe not. "You know em?"

"Seen 'em around once or twice. That bracket on his truck is for a thermal camera...like ours."

I couldn't see the truck but remember it driving past us once in between the breakfast and brunch rib slabs. On the whole the campsite isn't big, but it's big enough that another party could keep relatively hidden from another one until they had to leave for supplies and traverse the only road in and out. "Competition?"

"Nah. Just want to give them a wide berth." Randy checks his camera settings again before taking the meat off the grill and pulling a large carton of coleslaw out of the cooler. I like slaw. "We'll eat now, head out after they do."

I don't like that course of action. I've always been the kid who couldn't sit still and I'd been sitting on my ass all day. I need to do something. Anything. But no. We sit and eat and sure enough the other party-an adult male and two teens-drive past as the sun disappears and twilight takes over. I clean the plates, take them to the closest trash can, put the fire out, and get my gear ready to prod the boys into action, but they move like frozen molasses. There was no urgency and Andy keeps staring in the direction of the other party's campsite and ridge behind it without saying a word. Randy too. Both are silent and spend an inordinate amount of time sitting on their pop-up chairs. Night is almost on us and the last thing I want is to fuck around with gear in the dark. Why didn't they...

"There," Andy whispers.

"What?"

"Shhh," Randy says low as he stares into where the fire is now smoldering. We were in a triangle, me standing, Randy and Andy sitting. Randy thumbs a small remote. A camera remote. I look at his Canon still perched on the tripod, a tiny red light blinking on the back. It was still aimed toward the west at a ridge where...

"Jesus fuck!" I say.

"Keep it down," Randy says quietly, his back to the ridge.

"But there's there's a..."

"I know."

"I think I just heard a cherry pop," Andy jokes. I've never been so completely consumed with fear in my life. Goosebumps run down my arms and back and I physically shudder. On the ridgeline half covered by a tree but silhouetted clearly against the twilight is a massive figure swaying back and forth almost like an old man trying to stand. We're at least half a football field away and it looks gargantuan. It was Kareem Abdul Jabbar's height and Lou Ferigno's width. With no way to stop myself I step toward it.

"Don't."

"I have to know." Another step and it takes off running down the ridge away from us.

"He's running!" Andy says, jumping out of his steak coma and grabbing the backpack at his feet. In one fluid movement Randy rises, turns, grabs the camera off the tripod and is in a full sprint to the ridgeline with Andy and I right behind. They're as nimble as ever and we cover the distance a helluva lot faster than you would expect three middle aged fat asses to as the adrenaline pushes and discovery pulls us forward. Fear, nausea, and excitement swirled into a cocktail of manliness.

We hit the top of the ridge where we last saw it and stop. Randy holds the camera up to his face and scans down the hill in the direction it fled. "I got nothing."

"Well let's go!" I say charging down the hill, Sir Winston's words guiding me. *"One ought never to turn one's back on a threatened danger and try to run away from it. Never run away from anything. Never!"*

A rock slams into a tree ten feet to my right stopping me dead in my tracks. I was rushing across an open courtyard toward an Iraqi door when a shot rings out. The common denominator in each situation being an unknown adversary who can see you while you can't see it...with the potential to end your life.

"Yeah, you don't wanna do that," Randy says still scanning with the camera.

"Did it just throw a fucking rock at us?!"

"You're lucky he didn't hit you," Andy says as he examines the spot next to the tree where the beast must have been standing. "Here we go."

I quickly move back up the hill to him. Randy's face stays glued to the camera with its night vision capability.

Andy's thick arm is extended and he points to a spot on the ground where I see nothing. And then a toe. And another. Giant toe prints lightly embedded next to the tree in some soft clay like the animal had spun and run quickly, probably when some idiot spooked it. "Tell me again how they're not harmful to humans," I say looking at the sheer size of the smeared footprint and remembering how large it was silhouetted against the skyline.

"Let's get back," Randy says turning to the campsite. "He's not coming back anytime soon." Andy follows suit.

"Don't you want to go after it?"

"Do you? It nearly crushed your head with that rock."

Very valid point. Whatever it was scared me, but at the same time I hadn't come out here and sat around all day just to leave without answers. Something was out there, close even, it haunted me and I had only gotten a glimpse of it. We couldn't do nothing.

"Don't worry," Randy says. "He's not done. That one's too curious."

And then I get it. Randy was drawing it in the whole time. He'd learned to think like one of them. We didn't walk all over Oklahoma last night to find a Sasquatch. We did it to get their attention. We didn't cook bacon, eggs, burgers, and ribs all day for our dining pleasure, but theirs. It's one of the basic tenets of combined arms warfare: know your enemy. And Randy knew his. But that also meant that I'd spoiled the ambush. Impatience was my undoing…and theirs as well. Dumbass.

Not even halfway back to the tents a knock echoes through the woods followed by another mere seconds later. "There we go," Andy says with a smile. For thirty agonizing minutes I sat on a tiny tripod chair breathing slowly through my nose to bring my heart rate down and struggling with the irrationality of what I'd just seen. Was it real or was it a man in an ape suit and Randy was elaborately punking me? Was this the new frontier where everything I'd worked so hard to understand about life was suddenly and savagely set on its head? It was my personal double rainbow and I struggled to find it's meaning. The universe rewarded me with the silence I needed to think but I hated it. I was lost in my own madness. The worst place in the world. Nothing happened. In the crucial minutes after this shocking experience what I needed were answers but all I got was Randy and Andy saying "keep quiet so he comes back."

Finally a howl rattles through the pines. I've been deep in the woods when a red fox screamed a mating call and even deeper in the Florida swamps when an alligator did the same. Both scared the fucking bejesus out of me. This was worse. It was what I imagine a tribe of giant Howler monkeys in a cave sounds like and its haunting call seemed to carry on forever. It was unmistakable, so I give in to it, which scared me just as much as anything else, but what could I do? I saw it, heard it, and almost felt it when that rock narrowly missed me. Was this really happening? Was I really transforming into a believer at this very moment?

I didn't argue when Randy suggested we retreat to the cab of the truck. He didn't see a benefit in going out and looking for it and again adopted the most cruel of strategies...waiting. But patience was our best chance to leave with what we'd come for. Something was definitely out there and it was still interested in ripping us to shreds. At least that's what I thought it wanted.

Randy had replicated the conditions from his most successful encounter. He built a campsite sloppily strewn with the detritus of recreational lifestyle so any living creature with a sense of smell would be drawn to it. He waited for the target to come to us instead of vice versa. He refused to play by the rule of the woods and demanded that the encounter happen on his own terms.

But he hadn't accounted for one variable: me. I'd blown the trap. Not that Sasquatch would have waltzed down into the camp with us there and had a burger, but we probably could have gotten more footage had I kept my cool. Even worse I charged into the unknown and instead of getting the answers I wanted I had created more questions. I stewed in the broth of failure. Two silent hours later I was fully cooked.

The sun rose. It wasn't ideal, but I had something solid that told me the world as I knew it was not as well defined as higher education had led me to believe. There are still things out there to be discovered, boundaries to push, battles to win, a final frontier to go where no man has gone before. I could leave Oklahoma with a little more passion than when I arrived.

On the way out we told Ranger Bill we didn't experience anything. Total lie. He came across as an unsuspecting dimwit but I couldn't look at him that way after Randy's assertion that he might actually be the zookeeper tending to a herd of secret Bigfeet. I imagine a higher power would have to entrust that responsibility to only the best and brightest individual possibly with a background in primate study and covert ops. I stared at Ranger Bill trying to determine if that was the man he really was under the affable, non-threatening, boy next door demeanor. All I saw was a Park Ranger.

"You charged that thing like nothing I've ever seen," Randy laughs as we watch the sketchy video footage at his house.

"I'm a fighter, brother. If I don't have an enemy my soul atrophies."

"Big word."

"You're no idiot. You know what it means."

We watched it five, six, seven more times looking hard for anything we'd missed. It never got old. I loved the thrill of the chase especially from this comfy couch. "Dude, I'm sorry I spoiled the..."

"Quit apologizin'. It all comes out in the wash."

"Yeah but there's a big difference between pouncing on an opportunity and rushing into a mistake. I've done both."

"Well, either way that was fun as shit huh?" He rose to go to the kitchen. I wanted to talk more, but the constant flow of kids through the room stifled me. It's not like when we were younger and guys could go out and be guys and talk over beers and cigars. As long as I'd known him everything was different now. I understood him and wondered what it would take for others to understand me. I'm sure as hell not taking anyone Sasquatch hunting.

SOMEDAY
I can't wait to get there

Someday I'm gonna...

You're gonna what? You keep saying that, but do you ever do it? Does someday ever come? Do you ever do the things in your someday? To me Someday is a small town on the horizon that you can't reach because your car runs out of gas and you complain like everyone else that it's 'just my luck.'

Someday has an exclusive population of over-achievers. The mailboxes in Someday have names like Gates, Trump and Pitt and I'd like to think there's a townhome or condo waiting for me, but then I stop dreaming and get back to work, because that's the way Someday works.

But not just yet, I want to imagine some more.

In Someday my wife cooks me a fantastic breakfast that drives my libido to take her on the kitchen island. Twice. In Someday there's a new car in my driveway that changes more often than Charlie Sheen's Redbox account. Today's pick is a Jaguar XKR convertible. Midnight Blue with the upgraded premium leather package. I grab a Tag Heuer from my watch collection and roar the big V12 out of the driveway, narrowly missing Hillary Swank and Nikki Cox as they jog past in skimpy outfits and wave.

Did I remember to lock my door? Are you kidding? There's no crime in Someday. Criminals are executed with extreme prejudice and in public. It's a great deterrent. In Someday I can take a brief ski in my Speedo's at the local mountain and then head to Someday Beach to tan my perfect abs. There's no such thing as cancer here, but we do have a playful ass-slapping law that makes it more legal than an NFL game. I'm so glad I voted for Mayor Schwarzenegger.

Partisan politics doesn't get in the way of progress and tolerance is universal. The schools are clean and safe, no one is required to attend sensitivity training, and no one's heard of a support group. Driving through Someday you'll notice the dogs don't bark, there are no mullets, door-to-door salesmen, boy bands, chick-stealing back-stabbers, protests against violent sports, man-ponytails, spouse abuse, fanny packs, oversized RELAX shirts, or hot pink anything unless it's a neon sign on the casino where everyone wins.

Dinner is the fresh catch of the day that someone in a slicker dropped off at the house moments after his boat hit the dock. And though I have no idea who it was, I'm sure he was great eye candy for the wife, since she deserves something better to look at than me. Just wait until she sees our hot, new Spanish pool girl. Admiring beauty of the opposite sex is not only allowed in Someday, it's encouraged. Just don't think of cheating though; adulterers are castrated with a rusty knife and have their testicles sewn into their eyelids for all to see. Thank former mayor Charlton Heston for that.

In Someday I'll actually check the mail because it's not the worthless credit card offers, lawn service flyers, and real estate listings. In Someday we always get all-new, commercial-free episodes of House of Cards and Cosmos and watch them with a box of Girl Scout cookies that's been engineered to fight fat. The residents of Someday have the ability to choose for themselves and have banned huge marketing blitzes to sell them on what's good. In Someday, even Saturday Night Live is funny again.

In Someday my old Army buddies and I watch a game of rugby and talk with pride about our favorite players from the US team, who finally won a World Cup and got the general public to spell SCRUM correctly. It's the official sport in Someday because the athletes aren't spoiled whining schoolgirls going on strike over salary caps. People work hard, admit their failures and take responsibility here.

In Someday kids say things sincerely, like 'please,' 'thank you,' 'I love you daddy,' and 'It really wasn't my brother's fault your Cuban cigars got flushed down the toilet. I did it.'

Yeah, Someday...the elusive town where virtue and vice commingle, dreams come true, and hope is stricken from the vocabulary. I hope to see it...someday.

ABOUT THE AUTHOR

Kelly Crigger is an angry troll who lives under a bridge, eats goats that wander past, and throws their bones into the canyon of despair.